THE CIVIL WAR IN
SPOTSYLVANIA
COUNTY

Other books by Michael Aubrecht:

Onward Christian Soldier: The Spiritual Journey of Stonewall
Christian Cavalier: The Spiritual Legacy of JEB Stuart
The Southern Cross: A Civil War Devotional
Historic Churches of Fredericksburg: Houses of the Holy
You Stink! Major League Baseball's Terrible Teams and Pathetic Players

THE CIVIL WAR IN
SPOTSYLVANIA
COUNTY

CONFEDERATE CAMPFIRES AT THE CROSSROADS

MICHAEL AUBRECHT

Charleston London

THE
History
PRESS

Published by The History Press
Charleston, SC 29403
www.historypress.net

First published 2009

Cover image: *Letter from Home*, Mort Künstler. *Courtesy of Künstler Enterprises Ltd.*

Manufactured in the United States

ISBN 978.1.59629.696.1

Library of Congress Cataloging-in-Publication Data

Aubrecht, Michael.
The Civil War in Spotsylvania County : Confederate campfires at the crossroads /
Michael Aubrecht.
p. cm.
Includes bibliographical references.
ISBN 978-1-59629-696-1
1. Spotsylvania County (Va.)--History, Military--19th century. 2. Spotsylvania County
(Va.)--Social conditions--19th century. 3. Virginia--History--Civil War, 1861-1865.
4. Soldiers--Virginia--Spotsylvania County--History--19th century. 5. Soldiers--
Confederate States--History. 6. Confederate States of America. Army--Military life.
7. Virginia--History--Civil War, 1861-1865--Social aspects. 8. United States--History--
Civil War, 1861-1865--Social aspects. I. Title.
F232.S8A93 2009
975.5'365--dc22
2009036541

This book is dedicated to my Uncle Jim Norris,
who is now watching over all of us.

CONTENTS

Acknowledgements   9
Introduction: Campfires at the Crossroads   11

Johnny Reb: Character Study of the Confederate Soldier   23
Camp Crusades: Religious Services,
    Chaplains and Prayer Meetings   45
Campfire Cooking: Campaign Diets and Not-So-Fine Dining   53
Colored "Confederates": Black Cooks, Body Servants and Slaves   60
Crime and Punishment: Executions,
    Courts-Martial and Humiliations   68
Silent Death: Dysentery, Disease and Sickness   75
Love Letters: Sweethearts, Wives and Last Words   82
On the Homefront: Civilian Memoirs and Experiences   91
Sons of Secession: Letters to the Family of Life on Campaign   99
Winter Quarters: Cabins, Markers and Snowball Fights   110
Rebel Recollections: News and Views from the Front Lines   122
Summation: The Bivouac in the Snow   133

Appendix: Army of Northern Virginia Camp Register:
    Listing of Confederate Units   137
Bibliography   151
About the Author   155
About the Cover   157

Acknowledgements

When The History Press commissioning editor John Wilkinson contacted me about doing a second book as part of the American Chronicles series, I must admit that I was both humbled and honored. My first title with THP, *Historic Churches of Fredericksburg: Houses of the Holy*, had been doing very well and I had already researched primary sources for a companion volume on the historic churches of Spotsylvania County. However, in anticipation of the upcoming American Civil War Sesquicentennial, the publisher was more interested in adding new books to the catalogue on the War Between the States, specifically about Spotsylvania County's experiences. I discussed the possibilities of tackling an original topic with John Hennessey, chief historian at the Fredericksburg & Spotsylvania National Military Park, and he suggested that I examine the far too neglected subject of Confederate encampments. John's colleagues at the NPS, Donald Pfanz and Eric Mink, later assisted me in the acquisition of photos and illustrations. Local historian and fellow National Civil War Life Foundation board member John Cummings was also extremely helpful, as was my friend and renowned painter Mort Künstler, who once again allowed me to use his wonderful artwork on the cover.

This topic proved to be a bit of a challenge, as the exact locations and numbers in these camps are relatively unknown. In fact, both the National Park Service and the Virginia Department of Historical Resources were unable to provide any information on specific campsites. Neither archaeological records nor relic hunter lists contained coordinates, and to this day, no definitive information has been made available to the public. Fortunately, our local NPS archives have a wonderful collection of personal letters, diary entries and military reports that present the secessionist's camp life and day-to-day hardships that were experienced in our area and neighboring counties. After spending several months collecting references, I was able to identify over fifty pieces from which to draw excerpts. As this book is presented in a chronicles format, I sought to make sure that it was more than just a good read. I intended for it to become a respected research tool for others. The following collection of letters, essays, diary entries and associated transcripts represents the voices of the common Confederate soldiers, as well as the civilians who witnessed their presence firsthand. I have also included a listing of units from the Army of Northern Virginia that were encamped in the area throughout the course of the war.

As with most books, the final copy that reaches the shelf represents the time and talents of many individuals and not just those of the author. This particular project was blessed from the beginning with a wonderful band of experts, visionaries and supporters. I could not have asked for a better assembly of people to help guide me along this journey, and they are to be credited with this study just as much, if not more, than I am. Thanks to all who contributed to this project in their own special way. At the risk of forgetting someone, I have decided to simply express my gratitude to all with whom I have had the privilege of working. Thank you my fellow historians, writers, editors, archivists, bloggers, researchers, publishers, reenactors, rangers, designers, curators and Civil War enthusiasts. Of course I want to recognize my wonderful family, from my beautiful and infinitely patient wife Tracy to my four children, Dylan, Madison, Kierstyn and Jackson, and my supportive parents, Tom and Linda Aubrecht. Your love and support means more than I could ever express in the written word.

Introduction

CAMPFIRES AT THE CROSSROADS

Camp life is becoming very monotonous at our present abode. Winter is near at hand, and our tents a very inadequate shelter for this cold clime. Wood too has become an object—far off and bad roads to haul it over. The cold winds, howling around us like evil spirits, admonish us to prepare for "worse coming."
—*James J. Kirkpatrick, 16th Mississippi Infantry, CSA*

O ften referred to as the "Crossroads of the Civil War," Spotsylvania County in central Virginia bore witness to some of the most intense fighting during the War Between the States. The nearby city of Fredericksburg and neighboring counties of Stafford, Orange and Caroline also hosted myriad historically significant events during America's "Great Divide."

Four major engagements took place in this region, including the Battles of Fredericksburg, Chancellorsville, Spotsylvania Court House and the Wilderness. Today, the hallowed grounds that make up the Fredericksburg & Spotsylvania National Military Park are the second largest of their kind in the country. In addition, the area remains home to many historic Civil War landmarks, including Chatham, Salem Church, the "Stonewall" Jackson Shrine and Ellwood Manor. Dozens of monuments and roadside markers dot the landscape, and more than 200,000 tourists visit the Fredericksburg and Spotsylvania region each year.

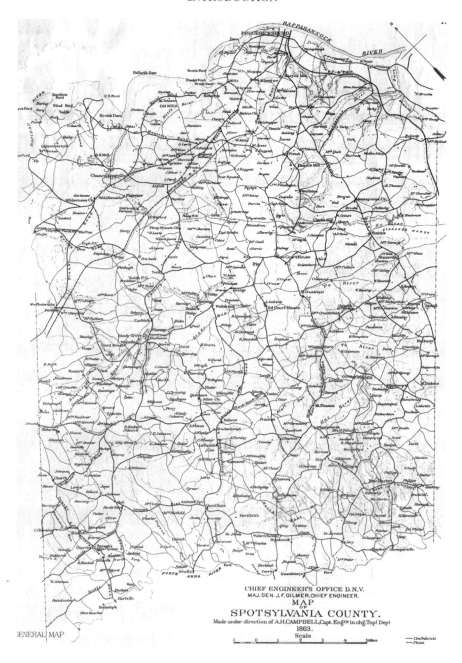

Wartime map of Spotsylvania County from the U.S. Army's Chief Engineer's Office of 1863. *Courtesy of the Spotsylvania Tourism Bureau.*

Similarly, from 1861 to 1865, hundreds of thousands of troops from both sides of the conflict marched through, fought at and camped in the woods and fields of Spotsylvania County and the surrounding area. The National Park Service christened the region "the Bloodiest Landscape in North America," stating that over a four-year period more than eighty-five thousand men were wounded and over fifteen thousand were killed. A number of exceptionally significant events also took place in the vicinity, including the first clash between Union general Ulysses S. Grant and Confederate commander General Robert E. Lee, as well as the first recorded skirmish between the Southern forces and U.S. Colored Troops.

This book focuses specifically on the Confederate encampments that spread across Spotsylvania County and the adjoining regions during the course of the Civil War. By using the testimonies of witnesses and words taken directly from published memoirs, diary entries and letters home, readers will be able to gain some insight regarding the day-to-day experiences of camp life for the Southern armies on campaign in the Old Dominion.

According to Spotsylvania County's official history, as presented by the tourism bureau:

> *Spotsylvania's roots extend back to 1721, when the colony of Virginia created a vast new county that stretched past the Blue Ridge Mountains. The county was named for Alexander Spotswood, lieutenant governor of the colony from 1710 to 1720. The City of Fredericksburg was formed from the county in 1728. Spotsylvania's many historic places include the following sites: a skirmish near the Rappahannock River between American Indians and a group led by Capt. John Smith; the first commercially successful ironworks in North America; a slave revolt attempted in the 1810s; and one of the nation's most productive pre-1849 gold mines. The county is probably best-known for the battles fought on its soil during the Civil War. Because of Spotsylvania's strategic location between the Confederate and Union armies, several major battles were fought in the county, including ones at Chancellorsville, the Wilderness, Fredericksburg, and Spotsylvania Court House, one of the bloodiest battles of the war. More than 100,000 troops from both sides died in Spotsylvania.*

The nearby town of Fredericksburg blends almost seamlessly into the county's landscape. Its authorized biography states:

> *The City of Fredericksburg was established by an act of the Virginia General Assembly in 1728, on land originally patented by John Buckner and Thomas*

Royston of Essex County in 1681. It was named for Frederick, Prince of Wales (1707–51), eldest son of King George II of Great Britain and father of King George III. Its older streets still bear the names of members of the British royal family. Located at the falls of the Rappahannock River, Fredericksburg flourished as a regional marketplace and prosperous seaport before the American Revolution. Although the Fredericksburg region is steeped in over 300 years of history, it is the area's part in the Civil War that attracts most of the visitors today. The City of Fredericksburg is strategically located midway between Washington D.C. and Richmond, Virginia. The City of Fredericksburg was a major objective for both sides during the Civil War. The city changed hands at least seven times and is the site of some of the most intense and crucial battles of the war.

Both locations, in addition to the surrounding counties of Stafford, Orange, Caroline and others, acted as major campsites and stationing locations for thousands of troops from both the Federal and Confederate armies.

Topics in this book include the construction and configuration of winter quarters, daily troop activities, church services, drills and assignments, foraging and supply acquisition, games and entertainment, crimes and punishment, servants, slaves and civilian aid, as well as personal reminiscences of missions and engagements. In addition, an intimate look into the family lives of several soldiers is revealed through their personal correspondence with loved ones who were left behind on the homefront.

Camp life for the common soldier during the Civil War was a mixture of a blessing and a curse. Off the battlefield, these encampments afforded a temporary sense of safety and security. They were also a bastion of boredom, and troops passed the time playing chess, singing songs and participating in a relatively new recreational activity called "baseball." At the same time, many soldiers fell victim to the indulgences of army life that included gambling, thievery, intoxication and prostitution. Thousands of men died of disease and dysentery from poor living conditions, and the scarring that was left behind on the land from camping armies proved to be just as destructive as the battles themselves.

Most soldiers in the field, regardless of their virtue, wrote constantly to reassure their friends and family, or simply to stay abreast of what was going on in their absence. As a result, there is a tremendous quantity of recorded memories available on life (and death) in these canvas communities. Enlisting with visions of glory, many of these men never expected to be away from their families for a long period of time, and few could have predicted the hardships that they would experience. Confederate forces suffered significantly more as

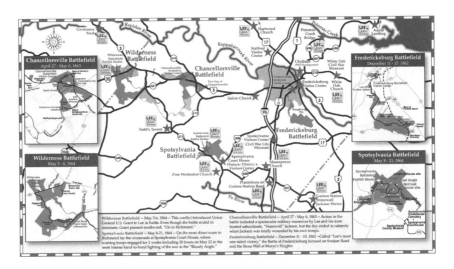

Map showing four major Civil War battlefields in the Fredericksburg/Spotsylvania area. *Courtesy of the Spotsylvania Tourism Bureau.*

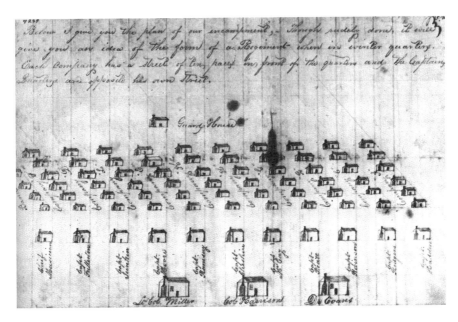

Sketch depicting the winter camp of the 1st South Carolina Rifles in Spotsylvania, 1864. *Courtesy of the University of South Carolina.*

Illustration from *Harper's Weekly* depicting Southern troops passing the time while camped in Virginia. *Courtesy of the Lee Foundation.*

the war dragged on, due to a rapidly depleting supply of military resources and basic life-sustaining necessities.

The broad demographic of these secessionists crossed all lines of society, which included everyone from privileged slave owners to poor farm boys. From a frustrated infantryman who described the monotony of his days like this: "The first thing in the morning is drill. Then drill a little more. Then drill, and lastly drill," to Confederate general Braxton Bragg, who commented on the debauchery of vices when he said, "We have lost more valuable lives at the hands of whiskey sellers than by the balls of our enemies," they all served in the same army and tented together regardless of their station.

Fortunately, we still have the written recordings of these soldiers who unknowingly preserved their own legacies by hand. Some pieces in this book were obviously penned early on as they bragged proudly about serving the "Cause." Others were composed long after they had become disenchanted with the war. Many of them were bittersweet as they captured the last chronicles of homesick husbands and fathers who later fell on the battlefield.

Due to inconsistent record keeping and the fact that most of the official records for the Confederate States of America were destroyed during the fall of Richmond in 1865, there is no definitive number that accurately represents the strength of the Southern army. Troop estimates range from 500,000 to 2,000,000 men who were involved at any time during the war. Reports from the War Department began at the end of 1861, indicating 326,768 men; in 1862 with 449,439 men; in 1863 with 464,646 men; in 1864 with 400,787 men; and the last report indicated 358,692 men. An estimate of enlistment throughout the war was 1,227,890 to 1,406,180.

Confederate general Robert E. Lee's Army of Northern Virginia is estimated to have had about 75,000 troops in its ranks during the Battles of Fredericksburg and Chancellorsville and about 62,000 during the Overland Campaign, which included engagements at Spotsylvania Court House and the Wilderness. Therefore, one could estimate roughly that anywhere between 62,000 and 75,000 soldiers were stationed or encamped around the region from 1861 to 1865. These numbers pale in comparison when measured against the 135,000 Federal troops that were said to be stationed and/or camped in the neighboring Stafford County.

The exact locations of many of these Confederate camps remain unknown, but the winter quarters for the South's more senior commanders are recorded and marked prominently. These include the headquarters of General Lee, General Longstreet and General Stuart. Other locations of campsites include the grounds of the Spotsylvania Court House and

Stone marker identifying Lee's headquarters near Zion United Methodist Church in Spotsylvania. *Courtesy of the Spotsylvania Tourism Bureau.*

along the Lee's Hill area near Massaponax. For many soldiers, who simply opened their letters with "camped near Fredericksburg," the meaning of "near" could mean anywhere in the Spotsylvania Court House or the surrounding region.

Many of the excerpts in this book were taken from the bound volumes collection at the Fredericksburg & Spotsylvania National Military Park Service archives. Some are quoted from the original Southern Historical Society Papers. Other pieces cite quotes found in the postwar autobiographies of those who survived. They have been credited in all instances, and the original wording has not been corrected or modified in any way, in order to preserve the integrity of the original documents.

Readers will likely note a distinct difference between the writing and spelling of those individuals who were schooled and those who were uneducated. Many of these transcripts contain poor grammar, no punctuation, atrocious spelling and primitive composition. They also contain an honesty and sincerity that could only be presented through mirroring their original structure. All of them provide an intimate look into the lives of those stationed at Confederate encampments in and around Spotsylvania County.

Judge J.W. Stevens, a member of Hood's Texas Brigade in the Army of Northern Virginia, recalled the average Confederate soldier's camp experiences in his recollections titled *Reminiscences of the Civil War*. He wrote:

From the time we got our lines formed around the city of Fredericksburg we had all been informed, and it was understood by every man in the ranks, that whenever we heard a cannon fire in the city it would signal the enemy's advance. About the 6th or 7th of December we had a very severe snow storm. The weather was intensely cold. I suppose the snow was a foot or more in depth, but we were quite comfortable in our dog houses, and while the snow covered the ground, we were excused from drill—hence we had little to do but except keep up the fires and cook our rations, which were now very good, and we would supplement them by going to the butcher grounds and get a beef liver or beef head. You have no idea what fine eating there is on a beef's head. We would take the head and skin it nicely and chip the meat off in pieces—two, three or four inches in diameter and usually a half an inch thick, out it in a skillet, and fill the skillet with water, then put the lid on, then a fire both on top and under it. First it was a stew, and then a bake. It was very fine to our soldier appetites. On the morning of the 11th of December when the thermometer was down about zero and the earth was covered with snow, as I lay comfortably in my little dog house and everything seemed as still as a grave yard, boom went

Left: General Robert E. Lee, commander of the Army of Northern Virginia. *Courtesy of the Library of Congress*.

Below: General Lee's headquarters flag was supposedly designed by his wife Mary to reflect the Biblical Ark of the Covenant. *Courtesy of the Museum of the Confederacy*.

the signal gun in the city about a mile away. The sound reverberated up and down the river and borne back upon the crisp chilled air it reached every ear of Lee's soldiery, conveying to us the information that Burnside was preparing to cross the river to give us battle. I called to my sleeping bunk mates to get up. In the short space of five minutes we are in line—a few minutes more we have a regiment formed, and we are moving out to take our places in the line of battle. Oh how cold—but we moved.

…In a day or two we moved back into the timber about a mile further than the position we occupy when we first get to Fredericksburg and prepare to spend the next sixty days in winter quarters, our friends—the enemy—occupying a similar position on the north side of the river. Here both armies remain until the 20th of February following. We at once begin to make ourselves as comfortable as possible each company dividing up into messes. These messes are usually composed of four to six men. We begin at once to erect our little dog houses. Now as I have promised to tell my young readers about the dog house, I guess I had as well do so here.

We select a tree about ten or twelve inches in diameter, being careful to get one with a long straight body, and that has the appearance of splitting well. We cut it up into cuts seven to ten feet long, according to the size of the dog house we want, which is governed by the number of men in the mess. We split the cuts up into slabs about eight inches thick; then we begin somewhat as you would to build a pig pen, building up one end (to the north) and the two sides, leaving the south end open. We build up about three feet high, then we set up a fork or post at the center of each end, and put a pole across for a ridge pole, or comb of the structure, and over this we place a covering of anything we can get—usually an old piece of tent cloth, drawing it tightly down to the logs or slabs on each side as tight as we can and making it fast. Then we close up the opening at the north end and close all the cracks, making it wind tight. We then rake up dry leaves and fill the dog house about ten inches deep with the leaves, which makes us a good warm bed. On these leaves we spread one blanket and use the remainder of our blankets for covering. Our fire is built at the open end, the reflection of the heat from the fire striking the top of the covering of this dog house obliquely, is thrown by reflection down upon our bedding, making it quite warm and comfortable. We keep up our fires in cold weather all day and pretty well all night. When not engaged in camp duty we set around our fires, talk and gossip and discuss the various fights, and the prospects of an early ending of the war, reading daily papers and writing letters home. Some of the boys, forgetting their early moral training at home, are off in a big game of poker and Confederate money is piled up in the regular gambling style, others are *visiting friends in other messes, companies or regiments and passing time off very pleasantly, considering the circumstances with which we are surrounded. I have never been able to detail everything in camp life as minutely as I might have done for the information of my young readers. The sole object of these sketches has been to give those who never saw an army camp an idea of every-day life in time of war, and yet I find it very hard to bring in everything.*

If you will give me your attention, I will give you a few of the items of routine when in camp: At about day-light we have what is called "revilee" (it's the sound of the drum if you don't know what it is,) a quick beat for about half a minute by the regimental drummer. This calls us up; we get up and put on our accoutrements and each company forms a line and the roll is called. Then we stack arms and go to work to prepare our breakfast. Then the surgeon of the regiment goes to the medical wagon, and all who need medicine of any kind report to him, and he prescribes for them. If you are too sick to go to the surgeon, he visits them at their quarters; this is called "sick call." Then about 9:30 a.m. the drill call is sounded and each company is formed. If it is a company drill, each company marched out to some suitable place and drills about two or two and one-half hours. If it is a battalion drill, the regiment forms on the color line, and the whole regiment marches out into an open field, and the colonel, or some regimental officer, drills the regiment. Occasionally we have a brigade drill by the brigade commander, and on some special occasions we have what is called "review"—this may be either division or corps review. On these occasions the generals are out in full dress, and the troops are supposed to have on their best "bib and tucker." Now, so much in as few words as possible regarding the drill. After the first year we were seldom required to drill in the afternoon, tho' we did sometimes. About an hour before sundown in the evening we hold what is called "dress parade." In this the regiment is formed on the color line, and after being properly dressed, any orders or information that is desired to be read to the troops, is read by the adjutant in a loud and distinct voice. I remember one evening it was read out to us that one of our regiment had been found guilty of some offense that the articles of war punished by whipping. The crime, as I now remember, was being absent for some time without leave. Perhaps his offense was without justification, and I expect he deserved a very severe punishment, but the order went on to announce his trial and conviction by a court martial, to be whipped on the naked back in front of the regiment on the color line, and that the same was to take place two or three days in the future; that he was to be stripped to the waist and thirty-nine lashes laid on his bare back. Now he had been all the time a good soldier, brave and manly.

No man in the regiment felt willing to excuse his offense without some sort of punishment, but we felt then and there that he ought not, and should not, be whipped, and inside of 30 minutes from the time the parade was dismissed, I think everyman in the regiment had expressed a determination that he should not receive the whipping. I never heard any more of it. It may have been that the authorities never intended that he should be whipped at first, but simply wished to give some of the boys a scare, who occasionally offended in that way. That same man is today prominent in one of the counties in the Northeast Texas, and was a State Senator a few years ago.

We had divine services as often as it was convenient to do so. Our regiment had no regular chaplain. This writer enjoyed the distinction of being the only preacher in the regiment (So far as I now remember.) We very often had some kind of service for the boys, either in efforts to preach or a prayer meeting, and it is a source of comfort to me to this day to remember that frequently, at the close of a hard day's march, some officer from some other company in the regiment would have a light built and send for "Company K's preacher," as they called me, to come and hold meetin' for 'em. We had one or two other preachers in the brigade who would sometimes preach for us. Now you have a good idea of how the daily routine of duties go off when we are in camp.

Johnny Reb

Character Study of the Confederate Soldier

*The Confederate soldier was peculiar in that he was ever ready to fight,
but never ready to submit to the routine duty and discipline of the camp or
the march.*
—*Carlton McCarthy, Richmond Howitzers Artillery, CSA*

The life of a Confederate soldier was fraught with both dedication and despair. Unlike their Northern counterparts, troops enlisting in the Southern forces were typically not as well outfitted and had a difficult time acquiring basic necessities such as food and proper clothing, especially as the war dragged on. Much like the volunteers in the Continental army during the American Revolution, Confederate soldiers were to be supplied by their individual states, not by the secessionist government. This led to a lack of organization and uniformity among the ranks. Some soldiers did not possess warm jackets for the winter months and many went without boots, or any footwear, for that matter. Most men traveled light and carried a simple pack consisting of a rolled blanket, canteen (usually wooden), a small cooking kit with a tin cup and pan and a haversack that held rations and personal items such as playing cards.

The soldier usually carried an Enfield musket and kept his ammunition in a cartridge box that would be attached to his belt. If he was a believer, he would most likely have a small Bible or religious tracts on hand. Many men carried tobacco, whether they smoked or not, as it was a valuable trading commodity. In addition to being poorly supplied, Rebel troops were also poorly funded. Sometimes months would pass before they would receive monetary compensation for their services. This not only affected the soldier, but also loved ones who were dependent on that income for food and taxes. Sometimes relatives, as well as soldiers, would suffer from starvation, as the quality of life on the homefront was not much better than life in the camp.

In order to fully appreciate the day-to-day existence of the Southerner on campaign, one must first examine the mindset of the soldier himself. Veteran Carlton McCarthy, a private of the Second Company of the Richmond Howitzers, wrote a series of memoirs titled a "Detailed Minutiae of Soldier Life in the Army of Northern Virginia," which were published in the *Southern Historical Society Papers* in the 1870s. In them, he describes a variety of character traits, from the appearance and experiences of the average soldiers to their inevitable disenchantment with the romance and pageantry of war.

McCarthy's unit, the Richmond Howitzers, was present at all four battles in the area: Fredericksburg, Chancellorsville, the Wilderness and Spotsylvania. His battalion was encamped in the surrounding region on several occasions. McCarthy's insights into a soldier's life while on campaign in Spotsylvania County paint a portrait of dedication to duty in the midst of the direst of circumstances. Three of these papers follow:

Paper No. 1.—The Outfit Modified.
Southern Historical Society Papers 2, *no. 3, Richmond, Virginia (September 1876)*

With the men who composed the Army of Northern Virginia will die the memory of those little things which made the Confederate soldier peculiarly what he was.

The historian who essays to write the "grand movements" will hardly stop to tell how the hungry private fried his bacon, baked his biscuit and smoked his pipe; how he was changed from time to time by the necessities of the service, until the gentleman, the student, the merchant, the mechanic and the farmer were merged into a perfect, all enduring, never tiring and invincible soldier. To preserve these little details, familiar to all soldiers, and by them not thought worthy of mention to others, because of their familiarity, but still dear to them and always the substance of their "war talks," is the object of this paper.

The volunteer of 1861 made extensive preparations for the field. Boots, he thought, were an absolute necessity, and the heavier the soles and longer the tops the better. His pants were stuffed inside the tops of his boots, of course. A double breasted coat, heavily wadded, with two rows of big brass buttons and a long skirt, was considered comfortable. A small stiff cap, with a narrow brim, took the place of the comfortable "felt" or the shining and towering tile worn in civil life.

Then over all was a huge overcoat, long and heavy, with a cape reaching nearly to the waist. On his back he strapped a knapsack containing a full stock of underwear, soap, towels, comb, brush, looking glass, toothbrush, paper and envelopes, pens, ink, pencils, blacking, photographs, smoking and chewing tobacco, pipes, twine string and cotton strips for wounds and other emergencies, needles and thread, buttons, knife, fork and spoon, and many other things as each man's idea of what he was to encounter varied. On the outside of the knapsack, solidly folded, were two great blankets and a rubber or oilcloth. This knapsack, &c., weighed from fifteen to twenty five pounds, and sometimes even more. All seemed to think it was impossible to have on too many or too heavy clothes, or to have too many conveniences, and each had an idea that to be a good soldier he must be provided against every possible emergency.

In addition to the knapsack, each man had a haversack, more or less costly, some of cloth and some of fine morocco, and stored with provisions always, as though he expected any moment to receive orders to march across the great desert, and supply his own wants on the way. A canteen was thought indispensable, and at the outset it was thought very prudent to keep it full of water. Many, expecting terrific hand to hand encounters, carried revolvers, and even bowie knives.

Merino shirts (and flannel) were thought to be the right thing, but experience demonstrated the contrary.

In addition to each man's private luggage, each mess, generally composed of from five to ten men who were drawn together by similar tastes and associations, had its outfit, consisting of a large camp chest containing skillet, frying pan, coffee boiler, bucket for lard, coffee box, salt box, sugar box, meal box, flour box, knives, forks, spoons, plates, cups, &c., &c. These chests were so large that 8 or 10 of them filled up an army wagon, and were so heavy that two strong men had all they could do to get one of them into the wagon. In addition to the chest each mess owned an axe, water bucket, and bread tray. Then the tents of each company, and little sheet iron stoves, and stove pipe, and the trunks and valises of the company officers, made an immense pile of stuff, so that each company had a small wagon train of its own.

All thought money was absolutely necessary, and for awhile rations were disdained, and the mess supplied with the best that could be bought with the mess fund. Gloves were thought to be good things to have in winter time, and the favorite style was buck gauntlets with long cuffs.

Quite a large number had a "boy" along to do the cooking and washing. Think of it! a Confederate soldier with a body servant all his own, to bring him a drink of water, black his boots, dust his clothes, cook his corn bread and bacon, and put wood on his fire. Never was there fonder admiration than these darkies displayed for their masters.

Their chief delight and glory was to praise the courage and good looks of "Marse Tom," and prophesy great things about his future. Many a ringing laugh and shout of fun originated in the queer remarks, shining countenance and glistening teeth of this now forever departed character.

It is amusing to think of the follies of the early part of the war, as illustrated by the outfits of the volunteers. They were so heavily clad, and so burdened with all manner of things, that a march was torture, and the wagon trains were so immense in proportion to the number of troops, that it would have been impossible to guard them in an enemy's country. Subordinate officers thought themselves entitled to transportation for trunks and even mattresses and folding bedsteads, and the privates were as ridiculous in their demands.

This much by way of introduction. The change came rapidly and stayed not until the transformation was complete. Nor was the change attributable alone to the orders of the general officers. The men soon learned the inconvenience and danger of so much luggage, and as they became more experienced, vied with each other in reducing themselves to light marching trim.

Experience soon demonstrated that boots were not agreeable on a long march. They were heavy and irksome, and when the heels were worn a little one sided, the wearer would find his ankle twisted nearly out of joint by every unevenness of the road. When thoroughly wet, it was a laborious undertaking to get them off, and worse to get them on in time to answer the morning roll call. And so good, strong, broad bottomed and big flat heeled brogues or brogans succeeded the boots, and were found much more comfortable and agreeable, easier put on and off, and altogether the most sensible.

A short waisted, single breasted jacket usurped the place of the long tail coat, and became universal. The enemy noticed this peculiarity, and called the Confederates gray jackets, which name was immediately transferred to those lively creatures, which were the constant admirers and inseparable companions of the Boys in Gray and Blue.

Caps were destined to hold out longer than some other uncomfortable things, but they finally yielded to the demands of comfort and common sense, and a good soft felt hat was worn instead. A man who has never been a soldier does

Members of the 1st Virginia Confederate Militia, Richmond Grays, CSA. *Courtesy of the Library of Congress.*

not know, nor indeed can know, the amount of comfort there is in a good soft hat in camp, and how utterly useless is a "soldier hat" as they are generally made. Why the Prussians, with all their experience, wear their heavy, unyielding helmets, and the French their little caps, is a mystery to a Confederate who has enjoyed the comfort of an old slouch.

Overcoats an inexperienced man would think an absolute necessity for men exposed to the rigors of a Northern Virginia winter, but they grew scarcer and scarcer. They were found a great inconvenience and burden. The men came to the conclusion that the trouble of carrying them hot days outweighed the comfort of having them when the cold day arrived. Besides they found that life in the open air hardened them to such an extent, that the changes in the temperature were not felt to any degree. Some clung to their overcoats to the last, but the majority got tired lugging them around, and either discarded them altogether, or trusted to capturing one about the time it would be needed. Nearly every overcoat in the army in the latter years was one of Uncle Sam's, captured from his boys.

The knapsack vanished early in the struggle. It was found that it was inconvenient to "change" the underwear too often, and the disposition not to change grew, as the knapsack was found to gall the back and shoulders, and weary the man before half the march was accomplished. It was found that the better way was to dress out and out, and wear that outfit until the enemy's knapsacks or the folks at home supplied a change. Certainly it did not pay to carry around clean clothes while waiting for the time to use them.

Very little washing was done, as a matter of course. Clothes once given up were parted with forever. There were good reasons for this. Cold water would not cleanse them or destroy the vermin, and hot water was not always to be had…One blanket to each man was found to be as much as could be carried, and amply sufficient for the severest weather. This was carried generally by rolling it lengthwise, with the rubber cloth outside, tying the ends of the roll together, and throwing the loop thus made over the left shoulder with the ends fastened together hanging under the right arm.

The haversack held its own to the last, and was found practical and useful. It very seldom, however, contained rations, but was used to carry all the articles generally carried in the knapsack; of course the stock was small. Somehow or other, many men managed to do without the haversack, and carried absolutely nothing but what they wore and had in their pockets. The infantry threw away their heavy cap boxes and cartridge boxes, and carried their caps and cartridges in their pockets. Canteens were very useful at times, but they were as a general thing discarded. They were not much used to carry water, but were found useful when the men were driven to the necessity of foraging, for conveying buttermilk, cider, sorghum; &c., to camp. A good strong tin cup was found better than a canteen, as it was easier to fill at a well or spring, and was serviceable as a boiler for making coffee when the column halted for the night.

Revolvers were found to be about as useless as heavy lumber as a private soldier could carry, and early in the war were sent home to be used by the women and children in protecting themselves from insult and violence at the hands of the ruffians who prowled about the country shirking duty.

Strong cotton was adopted in place of flannel and merino, for two reasons. First, because easier to wash, and second, because the vermin did not propagate so rapidly in cotton as in wool.

Common white cotton shirts and drawers proved the best that could be used by the private soldier.

Gloves to any but a mounted man were found useless, worse than useless. With the gloves on, it was impossible to handle an axe well, or buckle harness, or load a musket, or handle a rammer at the piece. Wearing them was found to be simply a habit, and so, on the principle that the less luggage the less labor, they were discarded.

The camp chest soon vanished. The Brigadiers and Major Generals even found them too troublesome, and soon they were left entirely to the quartermasters and commissaries. One skillet and a couple of frying pans, a bag for flour or meal, another bag for salt, sugar and coffee, divided by a knot tied between, served the purpose as well. The skillet passed from mess to mess. Each mess generally owned a frying pan, but often one served a company.

The oilcloth was found to be as good as the wooden tray for making up the dough. The water bucket held its own to the last!

Tents were rarely seen. All the poetry about the "tented field" died. Two men slept together, each had a blanket and an oilcloth. One oilcloth went next to the ground. The two laid on this, covered themselves with two blankets, protected from the rain with the second oilcloth on top, and slept very comfortably through rain, snow or hail, as it might be.

Very little money was seen in camp. The men did not expect, did not care for, or get often any pay, and they were not willing to deprive the old folks at home of their little supply; so they learned: to do without any money.

When rations got short and were getting shorter, it became necessary to dismiss the darkey servants. Some, however, became company servants, instead of private institutions, and held out faithfully to the end, cooking the rations away in the rear, and at the risk of life carrying them to the line of battle to be devoured with voracity by their "young mahsters."

Reduced to the minimum, the private soldier consisted of one man, one hat, one jacket, one shirt, one pair of pants, one pair of drawers, one pair of shoes, and one pair of socks. His baggage was one blanket, one rubber blanket, and one haversack. The haversack generally contained smoking tobacco and a pipe and generally a small piece of soap, with temporary additions of apples, persimmons, blackberries, and such other commodities as he could pick up on the march.

The company property consisted of two or three skillets and frying pans, which were sometimes carried in the wagon, but oftener in the hands of the soldiers. The infantrymen generally preferred to stick the handle of the frying pan in the barrel of a musket, and so carry it.

The wagon trains were devoted entirely to the transportation of ammunition and commissary and quartermaster's stores, which had not been issued. Rations which had become company property, and the baggage of the men, when they had any, was carried by the men themselves. If, as was sometimes the case, three days rations were issued at one time and the troops ordered to cook them

Above, left: Brigadier General Henry Hopkins Sibley, inventor of the "Sibley Tent." *Courtesy of the Library of Congress.*

Above, right: General J.E.B. Stuart, inventor of the "Stuart's Lightning Horse Hitcher." *Courtesy of the Library of Congress.*

and be prepared to march, they did cook them, and eat them if possible, so as to avoid the labor of carrying them. It was not such an undertaking either, to eat three days rations in one, as frequently none had been issued for more than a day, and when issued were cut down one half.

The infantry found out that bayonets were not of much use, and did not hesitate to throw them, with the scabbard, away.

The artillerymen, who started out with heavy sabers hanging to their belts, stuck them up in the mud as they marched, and left them for the ordinance officers to pick up and turn over to the cavalry.

The cavalrymen found sabres very tiresome when swung to the belt, and adopted the plan of fastening them to the saddle on the left side, with the hilt in front and in reach of the hand. Finally sabres got very scarce even among the cavalrymen, who relied more and more on their short rifles.

No soldiers ever marched with less to encumber them, and none marched faster or held out longer.

The courage and devotion of the men rose equal to every hardship and privation, and the very intensity of their sufferings became a source of merriment. *Instead of growling and deserting, they laughed at their own bare feet, ragged clothes and pinched faces, and weak, hungry, cold, wet, worried with vermin and itch, dirty, with no hope of reward or rest, but each fighting on his own personal account, needing not the voice of any to urge them on, marched cheerfully to meet the well fed and warmly clad hosts of the enemy.*

Paper No. 2.—Romantic Ideas Dissipated
Southern Historical Society Papers 2, no. 5, Richmond, Virginia *(September 1876)*

To offer a man promotion in the early part of the war was equivalent to an insult. The higher the social position, the greater the wealth, the more patriotic it would be to serve in the humble position of a private; and many men of education and ability in the various professions, refusing promotion, served under the command of men greatly their inferiors, mentally, morally, and as soldiers. It soon became apparent that the country wanted knowledge and ability, as well as muscle and endurance, and those who had capacity to serve in higher positions were promoted.

Still it remained true, that inferior men commanded their superiors in every respect, save one—Rank; and leaving out the one difference of rank, the officers and men were about on a par.

It took years to teach the educated privates in the army that it was their duty to give unquestioning obedience to officers, because they were such, who were awhile ago their playmates and associates in business. It frequently happened that the private, feeling hurt by the stern authority of the officer, would ask him to one side, challenge him to personal combat, and thrash him well.

After awhile these rambunctious privates learned all about extra duty, half rations and courts martial. It was only to conquer this independent resistance of discipline that punishment or force was necessary. The privates were as willing and anxious to fight and serve as the officers, and needed no pushing up to their duty.

It is amusing to recall the disgust with which the men would hear of their assignment to the rear as reserves. They regarded the order as a deliberate insult, planned by some officer who had a grudge against their regiment or battery, who had adopted this plan to prevent their presence in battle, and thus humiliate them. How soon did they learn the sweetness of a day's repose in the rear!

Another romantic notion, which for awhile possessed the boys, was that soldiers should not try to be comfortable, but glory in getting wet, being cold, hungry and tired. So they refused shelter in houses or barns, and, "like true soldiers," paddled about in the mud and rain, thinking thereby to serve their country better.

The real troubles had not come, and they were in a hurry to suffer some. They had not long thus impatiently to wait, nor could they latterly complain of the want of a chance to "do or die."

Volunteering for perilous or very onerous duty was popular at the outset, but as duties of this kind thickened it began to be thought time enough when the "orders" were peremptory or the orderly read the "detail."

Another fancy idea was that the principal occupation of a soldier should be actual conflict with the enemy.

They didn't dream of such a thing as camping for six months at a time without firing a gun, or marching and countermarching to mislead the enemy, or driving wagons and ambulances, building bridges, currying horses, and the thousand commonplace duties of the soldier.

On the other hand, great importance was attached to some duties which soon became mere drudgery.

Some times the whole detail for guard—first, second and third relief—would make it a point of honor to sit up the entire night, and watch and listen as though the enemy might pounce on them at any moment, and hurry them off to prison. Of course they soon learned how sweet it was, after two hours' walking of the beat, to turn in for four hours! which seemed to the sleepy man an eternity in anticipation, but only a brief time in retrospect, when the corporal gave him a "chunk," and remarked, "Time to go on guard."

Everybody remembers how we used to talk about "one Confederate whipping a dozen Yankees." Literally true sometimes, but, generally speaking, two to one made hard work for the boys. They didn't know at the beginning anything about the advantage the enemy had in being able to present man for man in front and then send as many more to worry the flanks and rear. They learned something about this very soon, and had to contend against it on almost every field they won.

Wounds were in great demand after the first wounded hero made his appearance. His wound was the envy of thousands of unfortunates who had not so much as a scratch to boast, and who felt "small" and of little consequence before the man with a bloody bandage. Many became despondent and groaned as they thought that perchance after all they were doomed to go home safe and sound, and hear, for all time, the praises of the fellow who had lost his arm by a cannon shot, or had his face ripped by a sabre, or his head smashed with a fragment of shell. After awhile the wound was regarded as a practical benefit. It secured a furlough of indefinite length, good eating, *the attention and admiration of the fair, and, if permanently disabling, a discharge. Wisdom, born of experience, soon taught all hands better sense, and the fences and trees and ditches and rocks became valuable and eagerly sought after when "the music" of "minnie" and the roar of the "Napoleon" twelve pounders was heard.*

Death on the field, glorious first and last, was dared for duty's sake, but the good soldier learned to guard his life, and yield it only at the call of duty.

Only the wisest men, those who had seen war before, imagined that the war would last more than a few months. The young volunteers thought one good battle would settle the whole matter; and, indeed, after "first Manassas" many thought they might as well go home! The whole North was frightened, and no more armies would dare assail the soil of Old Virginia. Colonels and brigadiers, with flesh wounds not worthy of notice, rushed to Richmond to report the victory and the end of the war! They had "seen sights" in the way of wounded and killed, plunder, &c., and according to their views no sane people would try again to conquer the heroes of that remarkable day.

The newspaper men delighted in telling the soldiers that the Yankees were a diminutive race, of feeble constitution, timid as hares, with no enthusiasm, and that they would perish in short order under the glow of our Southern sun.

Any one who has seen a regiment from Ohio or Maine knows how true these statements were. And besides the newspapers did not mention the English, Irish, German, French, Italian, Spanish, Swiss, Portuguese and Negroes, who were to swell the numbers of the enemy, and as our army grew less make his larger. True, there was not much fight in all this rubbish, but they answered well enough for drivers of wagons and ambulances, guarding stores and lines of communication, and doing all sorts of duty, while the good material was doing the fighting.

Sherman's army, marching through Richmond after the surrender of Lee and Johnston, seemed to be composed of a race of giants, well-fed and well-clad.

Many feared the war would end before they would have a fair chance to "make a record," and that when "the cruel war was over" they would have to sit by, dumb, and hear the more fortunate ones who had "smelt the battle" tell to admiring home circles the story of the bloody field. Most of these "got in" in time to satisfy their longings, and "got out" to learn that the man who did not go, but "kept out" and made money, was more admired and courted than the "poor fellow" with one leg or arm less than is "allowed."

It is fortunate for those who "skulked" that the war ended as it did, for had the South been successful, the soldiers would have been favored with every mark of distinction and honor, and they "despised and rejected" as they deserved to be.

While the war lasted it was the delight of some of the stoutly built fellows to go home for a few days, and kick and cuff and tongue lash the able bodied bombproofs. How coolly and submissively they took it all! How "big" they are now!

The rubbish accumulated by the hope of recognition burdened the soldiers nearly to the end.

England was to abolish the blockade and send us immense supplies of fine arms, large and small. France was thinking about landing an imperial force in Mexico, and marching thence to the relief of the South. But the "Confederate yell" never had an echo in the Marseillaise, or "God save the Queen," and Old Dixie was destined to sing her own song without the help even of "Maryland, my Maryland." The "war with England," which was to give Uncle Sam trouble and the South an ally, never came.

Those immense balloons which somebody was always inventing, and which were to sail over the enemy's camps dropping whole cargoes of explosives, never "tugged" at their anchors or "sailed majestically away."

As discipline improved and the men began to feel no longer simply volunteers, but enlisted volunteers, the romantic devotion which they had felt was succeeded by a feeling of constraint and necessity, and while the army was in reality very much improved and strengthened by the change, the soldiers imagined the contrary to be the case. And if discipline had been pushed to too great an extent, the army would have been deprived of the very essence of its life and power.

When the officers began to assert superiority by withdrawing from the messes and organizing "officer's messes," the bond of brotherhood was weakened; and who will say that the dignity which was thus maintained was compensation for the loss of personal devotion as between comrades?

At the outset the fact that men were in the same company put them somewhat on the same level and produced an almost perfect bond of sympathy, but as time wore on the various peculiarities and weaknesses of the men would show themselves, and each company, as a community, would separate into distinct circles as indifferent to each other, save in the common cause, as though they had never met as friends.

The pride of the volunteers was sorely tried by the incoming of conscripts— the most despised class in the army—and their devotion to company and regiment was visibly lessened. They could not bear the thought of having these men for comrades, and felt the flag insulted when claimed by one of them as "his flag." It was a great source of annoyance to the true men, but was a necessity. Conscripts crowded together in companies, regiments and brigades would have been useless—but scattered here and there among the good men, were utilized. And so, gradually, the pleasure that men had in being associated with others whom they respected as equals, was taken away and the social aspect of army life seriously marred.

The next serious blow to romance was the abolishment of election and the appointment of officers. Instead of the privilege and pleasure of picking out some good hearted, brave comrade and making him captain, the lieutenant was promoted without the consent of the men, or, what was harder to bear, some officer hitherto unknown was sent to take command. This was no doubt better for the service, but it had a serious effect on the minds of volunteer patriot soldiers, and looked to them too much like arbitrary power exercised over men who were fighting that very principle. They frequently had to acknowledge, however, that the officers were all they could ask, and in many instances became devotedly attached to them.

As the companies became decimated by disease, wounds, desertions and death, it became necessary to consolidate them, and so the social pleasures received another blow. Men from the same neighborhoods and villages, who had been schoolmates together,—were no longer in companies, but mingled indiscriminately with all sorts of men from anywhere and everywhere.

Those who have not served in the army as privates can form no idea of the extent to which such changes as those just mentioned effect the spirits and general worth of a soldier. Men who when surrounded by their old companions were brave and daring soldiers, full of spirit and hope, when thrust among strangers for whom they cared not and who cared not for them, became dull and listless, lost their courage and were slowly but surely "demoralized." They did, it is true, in many cases, stand up to the last, but they did it on dry principle—having none of that enthusiasm and delight in duty which once characterized them.

The Confederate soldier was peculiar in that he was ever ready to fight, but never ready to submit to the routine duty and discipline of the camp or the march. The soldiers were determined to be soldiers after their own notions, and do their duty for the love of it as they thought best. The officers saw the necessity for doing otherwise, and so the conflict was commenced and maintained to the end.

It is doubtful whether the Southern soldier would have submitted to any hardships which were purely the result of discipline, and, on the other hand, no amount of hardship clearly of necessity could cool his ardor. And in spite of all this antagonism between the officers and men, the presence of conscripts, the consolidation of commands, and many other discouraging facts, the privates in the ranks so conducted themselves that the historians of the North were forced to call them the finest body of infantry that was ever assembled. But to know the men, we must see them divested of all their false notions of soldier life, and enduring the incomparable hardships which marked the latter half of the war.

Paper No. 3.—On the March
Southern Historical Society Papers 3, no. 1, Richmond, Virginia
(January 1877)

It is a common mistake of those who write on subjects familiar to themselves, to omit that particularity of description and detailed mention which, to one not so conversant with the matters discussed, is necessary to a clear appreciation of the meaning of the writer. This mistake is all the more fatal when the writer lives and writes in one age and his readers live in another.

And so a soldier, writing for the information of the citizen, should forget his familiarity with the every day scenes of soldier life and strive to record even those things which seem to him too common to mention. Who does not know all about the marching of soldiers? Those who have never marched with them and some who have. The varied experience of thousands would not tell the whole story of the march. Every man must be heard before the story is told, and even then the part of those who fell by the way is wanting. Orders to move! Where? when? what for?—are the eager questions of the men as they begin their preparations to march. Generally nobody can answer, and the journey is commenced in utter ignorance of where it is to end. But shrewd guesses are made, and scraps of information will be picked up on the way. The main thought must be to "get ready to move." The orderly sergeant is shouting "fall in" and there is no time to lose. The probability is that before you get your blanket rolled up, find your frying pan, haversack, axe, &c., and "fall in" the roll call will be over, and some "extra duty" provided. No wonder there is bustle in the camp. Rapid decisions are to be made between the various conveniences which have accumulated, for some must be left. One fellow picks up the skillet, holds it awhile, mentally determining how much it weighs, and what will be the weight of it after carrying it five miles, and reluctantly, with a half ashamed, sly look, drops it and takes his place in ranks. Another having added to his store of blankets too freely, now has to decide which of the two or three he will leave. The old water bucket looks large and heavy, but one stout hearted, strong armed man has taken it affectionately to his care.

This is the time to say farewell to the bread tray, farewell to the little piles of clean straw laid between two logs, where it was so easy to sleep; farewell to those piles of wood, cut with so much labor; farewell to the girls in the neighborhood;

Studio portrait of unknown
Confederate soldier.
*Courtesy of the Little Rock
Historical Society.*

*farewell to the spring, farewell to "our tree" and "our fire" good bye to the fellows
who are not going, and a general good bye to the very hills and valleys.*

*Soldiers commonly threw away the most valuable articles they possessed.
Blankets, overcoats, shoes, bread and meat, all gave way to the necessities
of the march; and what one man threw away would frequently be the very
article another wanted and would immediately pick up. So there was not
much lost after all.*

*The first hour or so of the march was generally quite orderly—the men
preserving their places in ranks and marching with a good show of order;
but soon some lively fellow whistles an air, somebody else starts a song, the
whole column breaks out with roars of laughter, "route step" takes the place
of order, and the jolly singing, laughing, talking and joking that follows none
could describe.*

*Now let any young officer dare to pass along who sports a new hat, coat,
saddle, or anything new, or odd, or fine, and how nicely he is attended to.*

The expressions of good natured fun, or contempt, which one regiment of infantry was capable of uttering in a day for the benefit of passers by, would fill a volume. As one thing or another in the dress of the "subject" of their remarks attracted attention, they would shout, "Come out of that hat!—you can't hide in thar" "Come out of that coat, come out—there's a man in it" "Come out of them boots!!" The infantry seemed to know exactly what to say to torment cavalry and artillery.

If any one on the roadside was simple enough to recognize and address by name a man in the ranks, the whole column would kindly respond, and add all sorts of pleasant remarks, such as, "Halloa, John, here's your brother!" "Bill!!, oh Bill!!!, here's your ma!" "Glad to see you!—How's your grandma?" "How-dye do!" "Come out of that 'biled (boiled-clean) shirt'!"

Troops on the march were generally so cheerful and gay that an outsider looking on them as they marched would hardly imagine how they suffered. In summer time, the dust, combined with the heat, caused great suffering. The nostrils of the men, filled with dust, became dry and feverish, and even the throat did not escape. The "grit" was felt between the teeth, and the eyes were rendered almost useless. There was dust in eyes, mouth, ears and hair. The shoes were full of sand, and penetrating the clothes, and getting in at the neck, wrists and ankles, the dust, mixed with perspiration, produced an irritant almost as active as cantharides. The heat was at times terrific, but the men became greatly accustomed to it, and endured it with wonderful ease. Their heavy woollen clothes were a great annoyance. Tough linen or cotton clothes would have been a great relief; indeed, there are many objections to woollen clothing for soldiers even in winter. The sun produced great changes in the appearance of the men. Their skins were tanned to a dark brown or red, their hands black almost, and, added to this the long, uncut beard and hair, they too burned to a strange color, made them barely recognizable to the homefolks.

If the dust and the heat were not on hand to annoy, their very able substitutes were. Mud, cold, rain, snow, hail and wind took their places. Rain was the greatest discomfort a soldier could have. It was more uncomfortable than the severest cold with clear weather. Wet clothes, shoes and blankets; wet meat and bread; wet feet and wet ground; wet wood to burn, or, rather, not to burn; wet arms and ammunition; wet ground to sleep on, mud to wade through, swollen creeks to ford, muddy springs, and a thousand other discomforts attended the rain. There was no comfort on a rainy day or night except in "bed"—that is, under your blanket and oilcloth. Cold winds, blowing the rain in the faces of the men, increased the discomfort. Mud was often so deep as to submerge the horses and mules, and at times it was necessary for one man or more to extricate another from the mud holes in the road.

Marching at night, when very dark, was attended with additional discomforts and dangers, such as falling off bridges, stumbling into ditches, tearing the face and injuring the eyes against the bushes and projecting limbs of trees, and getting separated from your own company and hopelessly lost in the multitude.

Of course, a man lost had no sympathy. If he dared to ask a question, every man in hearing would answer, each differently, and then the whole multitude would roar with laughter at the lost man, and ask him "if his mother knew he was out?"

Very few men had comfortable or fitting shoes, and less had socks, and, as a consequence, the suffering from bruised and inflamed feet was terrible. It was a common practice, on long marches, for the men to take off their shoes and carry them in their hands or swung over their shoulder.

When large bodies of troops were moving on the same road the alternate "halt" and "forward" was very harassing. Every obstacle produced a halt and caused the men at once to sit and lie down on the road side where shade or grass tempted them, and about the time they got fixed they would hear the word "forward!" and then have to move at increased speed to close up the gap in the column.

Sitting down for a few minutes on a long march is pleasant, but it does not always pay. When the march is resumed the limbs are stiff and sore, and the man rather worsted by the rest.

About noon on a hot day, some fellow with the water instinct would determine in his own mind that a well was not far ahead, and start off in a trot to reach it before the column. Of course another followed and another, till a stream of men were hurrying to the well, which was soon completely surrounded by a thirsty mob, yelling and pushing and pulling to get to the bucket as the windlass brought it again and again to the surface. Impatience and haste soon overturn the windlass, spatter the water all around the well till the whole crowd is wading in mud, and now the rope is broken and the bucket falls to the bottom. But there is a substitute for rope and bucket. The men hasten away and get long slim poles, and on them tie, by their straps, a number of canteens, which they lower into the well and fill, and, unless, as was frequently the case, the whole lot slipped off and fell to the bottom, drew them to the top and distributed them to their owners, who at once threw their heads back, inserted the nozzles in their mouths and drank the last drop, hastening at once to rejoin the marching column, leaving behind them a dismantled and dry well. It was *in vain the officers tried to stop the stream making for the water, and equally vain to attempt to move the crowd while a drop remained accessible. Many who were thoughtful carried full canteens to comrades in the column who had not been able to get to the well, and no one who has not had experience of it knows the thrill of gratification and delight which those fellows knew when the cool stream gurgled from the battered canteen down their parched throats.*

In very hot weather, when the necessities of the service allowed it there was a halt about noon, of an hour or so, to rest the men and give them a chance to cool off and get the sand and gravel out of their shoes. This time was spent by some in absolute repose but the lively boys told many a yarn, cracked many a joke, and sung many a song between "halt" and "column forward!". Some took the opportunity, if water was near, to bathe their feet, hands and face, and nothing could be more enjoyable.

The passage of a cider cart (a barrel on wheels) was a rare and exciting occurrence. The rapidity with which a barrel of sweet cider was consumed would astonish any one who saw it for the first time, and generally the owner had cause to wonder at the small return in cash. Sometimes a desperately enterprising darkey would approach the column with a cart load of pies "so called." It would be impossible to describe accurately the taste or appearance of these pies. They were generally similar in appearance, size and thickness to a pale specimen of "Old Virginia" buckwheat cakes, and had a taste which resembled a combination of rancid lard and crab apples. It was generally supposed that they contained dried apples, and the sellers were careful to state that they had "sugar in 'em" and "was mighty nice." It was rarely the case that any "trace" of sugar was found, but they filled up a hungry man wonderfully. Men of sense, and there were many such in the ranks, were necessarily desirous of knowing where or how far they were to march, and suffered greatly from a feeling of helpless ignorance of where they were and whither bound—whether to battle or camp. Frequently, when anticipating the quiet and rest of an ideal camp, they were thrown, weary and exhausted, into the face of a waiting enemy, and at times, after anticipating a sharp fight, having formed line of battle and braced themselves for the coming danger, suffered all the apprehension and gotten themselves in good fighting trim, they would be marched off in the dryest and prosiest sort of style and ordered into camp, where, in all probability, they had to "wait for the wagon," and for the bread and meat therein, until the proverb, "Patient waiting is no loss," lost all its force and beauty.

Occasionally, when the column extended for a mile or more, and the road was one dense moving mass of men, a cheer would be heard away ahead and increasing in volume as it approached until there was one universal shout. Then some general favorite officer would dash by, followed by his staff, and explain the cause.

At other times, the same cheering and enthusiasm would result from the passage down the column of some obscure and despised officer, who knew it was all a joke, and looked mean and sheepish accordingly.

The men would generally help each other in real distress, but their delight was to torment any one who was unfortunate in a ridiculous way. If, for instance, a piece of artillery was fast in the mud, the infantry and cavalry passing around the obstruction would rack their brains for words and phrases applicable to the situation and most calculated to worry the cannoneers who, waist deep in the mud, are tugging at the wheels.

Brass bands, at first quite numerous and good, became very rare and the music very poor in the latter years of the war. It was a fine thing to see the fellows trying to keep the music going as they waded through the mud. But poor as the music was, it helped the footsore and weary to make another mile, and encouraged a cheer and a brisker step from the lagging and tired column.

As the men became tired, there was less and less talking, until the whole mass became quiet and serious. Each man was occupied with his own thoughts. For miles nothing could be heard but the steady tramp of the men, the rattling and jingling of canteens and accoutrements, and the occasional "close up, men,— close up!" of the officers. As evening came on, questioning of the officers was in order, and for an hour it would be, "Captain, when are we going into camp?" "I say, lieutenant! are we going to or to blank?" "Seen anything of our wagon?" "How long are we to stay here?" "Where's the spring?" Sometimes these questions were meant simply to tease, but generally they betrayed anxiety of some sort and a close observer would easily detect the seriousness of the man who asked after "our wagon," because he spoke feelingly as one who wanted his supper and was in doubt as to whether or not he would get it.

Many a poor fellow dropped in the road and breathed his last in the corner of a fence, with no one to hear his last fond mention of his loved ones. And many whose ambition it was to share every danger and discomfort with their comrades, overcome by the heat or worn out with disease, were compelled to leave the ranks, and while friend and brother marched to battle, drag their weak and staggering frames to the rear, perhaps to die, pitiably alone, in some hospital, and be buried as one more "Unknown."

An accomplished straggler could assume more misery, look more horribly emaciated, tell more dismal stories of distress, eat more and march further (to the rear), than any ten ordinary men. Most stragglers were real sufferers, but

Sibley Tents used by the United States Army. *National Archives.*

many of them were ingenious liars, energetic foragers, plunder hunters and gormandizers. Thousands who kept their place in ranks to the very end were equally as tired, as sick, as hungry and as hopeless as these scamps, but too proud to tell it or use it as a means of escape from hardship.

Enlisted men were not the only ones worthy of mention. One noteworthy commander, who was buried in the local Fredericksburg Confederate Cemetery, made a significant contribution to camp life that benefited soldiers on both sides of the conflict. Brigadier General Henry Hopkins Sibley invented a special tent configuration that was inspired by the teepee of a Comanche chief that he had visited in the mid-1850s while on duty at Fort Belknap in Texas. His plans featured a lightweight conical tent with a wood stove and a single center pole. The design enabled soldiers to heat their canvas quarters while venting the smoke out of the roof. This kept the interior of the tent both warm and dry.

The U.S. War Department adopted the shelter, and it was used by both sides in the Civil War and during the later Indian wars. Following the end of the Civil War, Sibley journeyed to Egypt for a brief stint before returning to the States and settling in Fredericksburg. Upon his arrival, he petitioned the federal government to pay him an estimated $100,000 in back royalties for his tent design. Due to his resignation from the army to join the Confederacy, Sibley unknowingly had forfeited any opportunities to receive pay for his creation. Confederate generals Dan Ruggles and Carter L. Stevenson attempted to assist Sibley, who died in 1886. He was buried in General Stevenson's plot and forgotten about until 1957, when his remains were relocated and properly marked.

General Sibley was not the only inventive commander with ties to the Fredericksburg and Spotsylvania areas. Cavalry commander J.E.B. Stuart, whose winter quarters were located along Route 1 near the Lee's Hill area, also designed an innovation that was adopted by the military. It remains as a rarely publicized episode in the life of this cavalier, as his flamboyant personality often eclipsed the creative ingenuity that he possessed. Years before the South's secession, J.E.B. served in the U.S. cavalry, which was conducting operations against Indian hostiles in the western territories. Following a winter spent at Fort Riley, Stuart's cavalry received its summer orders to protect settler routes along the Arkansas River. During this time, J.E.B. was granted a six-month furlough and returned to his home state of Virginia to establish his own homestead with his wife Flora.

While on leave, Stuart completed an invention devised to alleviate the problem of carrying a saber while on horseback. The attachment consisted of a simple brass hook that enabled a mounted soldier to hang his sword on the pommel of the saddle when dismounting to fight. Upon returning to his mount, the trooper could easily detach the weapon and return it to the side of his belt. Immensely proud and confident with his creation, "Stuart's Lightning Horse Hitcher," J.E.B. traveled to Washington to patent the device (P.N. 25684) and to present a demonstration of its benefits to the secretary of war. While waiting for his interview, Stuart was asked if he would take an important message regarding a raid to Lieutenant Colonel Robert E. Lee. Eager to do so, J.E.B. found his superior in Arlington, delivered the message and requested permission to accompany Lee as an aide. Impressed with the bravado of his young subordinate, the colonel granted his request. The mission later resulted in the Raid at Harpers Ferry. General Stuart would later command the cavalry in the Army of Northern Virginia and play a significant role in the victorious Battles of Fredericksburg and Chancellorsville.

CAMP CRUSADES

Religious Services, Chaplains and Prayer Meetings

There is a very general revival of religion going on in our Brigade at this time, baptizing every day. There are several churches in the surrounding country that our men go to every Sabbath.
—Simeon David, 14ᵗʰ North Carolina Infantry, CSA, from Camp Gregg near Guinea's Station

D uring the Civil War, an evangelical movement referred to as "the Great Revival" took place throughout the Army of the Confederacy. By the war's conclusion, it is estimated that at least 100,000 Southern troops claimed to be "born-again" after being introduced to the Biblical teachings of the Christian faith. These campaign conversions can be credited to the efforts of religious commanders such as General Thomas J. Jackson, who petitioned the government for the acquisition of chaplains to accompany the men into the field.

In a letter to the Southern Presbyterian General Assembly, Jackson stated, "Each branch of the Christian Church should send into the army some of its most prominent ministers who are distinguished for their piety, talents and zeal; and such ministers should labor to produce concert of action among chaplains and Christians in the army." He added,

Denominational distinctions should be kept out of view, and not touched upon. And, as a general rule, I do not think a chaplain who would preach denominational sermons should be in the army. His congregation is his

regiment, and it is composed of various denominations. I would like to see
no question asked in the army of what denomination a chaplain belongs to;
but let the question be, Does he preach the Gospel?

Protecting the sanctity of religious practices did not end with pious officers, as the entire Presbyterian denomination, as well as its contemporaries, was extremely concerned about the repercussions of the wartime climate. First and foremost was the inevitable splitting of the denominations following the South's secession. And although there appeared to be no immediate hostilities harbored by Christian leaders on either side, the fact remained that the political split in the country had also split the church. This resulted in a profound effect on virtually every aspect of its operations.

For example, up until the outbreak of the Civil War, the American Bible Society, based in New York, handled the production and distribution of most Protestant-based materials, including Bibles and tracts. After the conflict began, an entirely new system had to be formed in order to meet the needs of the Southern congregations. Many of these dilemmas were addressed in the minutes of the Presbyterian Church's General Assembly. One major point addressed the need to establish a new chapter of the Bible Society to shoulder the task of producing and distributing religious materials in the Confederate states. Another concern pertained to the issue of camp worship and the negative effects of military operations on the Sabbath.

Whenever possible, a schedule of morning and evening worship on Sundays, as well as Wednesday prayer meetings, was implemented. Often, preachers from nearby congregations would travel out to the camps to assist the attending chaplains or fill the gap as the need arose. One of the most popular ministers in the Fredericksburg region was the Presbyterian Church's Reverend Tucker Lacy, who routinely led the services, which were often attended by General Lee and his staff. Reverend Lacy's energizing speeches quickly became a popular event for saved and unsaved soldiers alike, who are said to have attended his camp sermons by the thousands. Many of these converts, as well as practicing believers, shared their newfound faith with their loved ones back home.

Letter from General Thomas "Stonewall" Jackson, Second Corps, Army of Northern Virginia, to the Presbyterian General Assembly:

Near FREDERICKSBURG VA
April 27th 1863

DEAR COLONEL, I am much gratified to see that you are one of the delegates to the General Assembly of our Church and I write to express the hope that something may be accomplished by you at the meeting of that influential body towards repealing the law requiring our mails to be carried on the Christian Sabbath. Recently I received a letter from a member of Congress (the Confederate Congress at Richmond) expressing the hope that the House of Representatives would act upon the subject during its present session; and from the mention made of Colonel Chilton and Mr. Curry of Alabama, I infer that they are members of the committee which recommends the repeal of the law. A few days since I received a very gratifying letter from Mr. Curry, which was voluntary on his part, as I was a stranger to him, and there had been no previous correspondence between us. His letter is of a cheering character, and he takes occasion to say that divine laws can be violated with impunity neither by governments nor individuals. I regret to say that he is fearful that the anxiety of members to return home, and the press of other business will prevent the desired action this session. I have said thus much in order that you may see that Congressional action is to be looked for at the next meeting of Congress; hence the importance that Christians act promptly, so that our legislators may see the current opinion before they take up the subject. I hope and pray that such may be our country's sentiment upon this and kindred subjects that our statesmen will see their way clearly. Now appears to me an auspicious time for action as our people are looking to God for assistance.

Very truly your friend,
TJ JACKSON

Letter from Jo Shaner of the Rockbridge Artillery to his parents:

Camp near Hamilton's Crossing
June 4th/63
Dear Mother,
As I have not writen to you or father since I left home I will try and write you both a few lines this morning we are still encamped near Hamilton's crossing but we got orders yesterday evening to cook two days rashons and to be redy to march at a moments warning and I think it is likely that we will march at

Left: General Thomas J. "Stonewall" Jackson, confederate commander and Presbyterian deacon. *Courtesy of Virginia Military Institute.*

Below: Field sketch depicting a prayer service at a Confederate camp. *Courtesy of the Library of Congress.*

any time. William McClintic got back to the company a few days ago he has bin at home sick he brought down with him a black boy to cook for our Mess. I recived a letter from Liza and Becca od a few days ago but I had writen a letter to them just the day before and so I will not write to them now untill they write to me again. They told me that Sarah ann had writen me a letter but I did not get it yet. Tell Liza and Becca that when they direct letters to me not to forget to direct them to the 1ˢᵗ Rockbridge Artillery in care of capt Graham General Ewell care for the last letter they wrote to me they directed it just in care capt Graham and there is more than one capt Graham in the army. I told Liza and Becca in my last letter that there was a meeting going on in the company and that men are taking a greate interest in the meetings and that meeting has still bin agoing on and I am happy to say that the Lord has bin doing greate work for us there has bin some 20 or more that has come forward and made a public profeshion that they intended to follow Christ and I supose that you both will be glad to hear that I have not bin left out of that number. Yes by the help of the Lord I intend to lead a new life I fell as though I was a new man some 10 or 12 of that number joined the church capt Graham also expressed a desire to become a member of the church. I hope that this good work may continue until every man in our company may become a Christian and oh what a happy company we would have then Just think of a company of all Christians there is the majority of our company now Christians I do not believe that I ever told you all about the prayers meetings we had in our company this last winter and spring we wold have them three times a week we did not think then that they ware doing any good but now we can see the good they did and now we still continue them and hope to do so as long as we are a company the Rev Mr Lacy comes over to preach to us very often he is the Chief Chaplain of our core, and preaches at the head quarters every Sunday and he seems to take greate interest in our company there was another man died that belonged to our company the other day in Richmond in the Hospital from a wound he recived in the last battle we had here he makes the 20th man that we have had kill in our company there has bin but few companies that has lost many men. Well I must soon close my letter I expect to send this letter by Mr Wright he is here now please excuse bad writing please write and tell Liza and Becca to write to me soon nothing more at present fondly remain you true son
Jo Shaner
to Father and Mother

Excerpts of letters from John McDonald of the 13th Mississippi Infantry to his wife:

Fredericksburg, VA
February the 28th, 1863
Dear Susan I am still awaiting with impatience for the expected letter I have not received a line since the letter that Crump brought dated feb. the 4th. I am getting uneasy about you and matters at home. Susan, there is one blessing of God that I can bost of at this time and that is I am in good health if it only pleases God to continue it with me. Susan there has been and is yet a great Camp meeting going on in our Brigade night and day for more than a week. they have got up a great revival among the soldiers I am a shame to say that I did not attend untill last night it was a warm meeting and a good many mourners and some joined the Church. it looked odd to see so many men and few ladies. the soldiers made the old Church ring melodious with the songs of praise to God who is the soldiers friend. Although soldiers have a rough row to weed. I never saw better attention paid to preaching as I recollect of in my life it seemed that the Lord really was there among our Mississ troops it seemed as if they had turned against the Devil, as well as, Lincoln, and with the help of God conquer both. I stood back and felt unworthy to be one of Gods soldiers. O dear Susan pray with all your power for you and for me and that this cruel and uncalled for war may soon close and let wearied soldiers return to their homes and dear ones. I still have no news to write that would interest you. Martin and Willis are well. Susan I weighed myself a few days ago. I weighed 138 pounds 10 pounds over my usual weight. You recollect that you Fannie and myself weighed last summer. I weighed 125 pounds and you 135 and Fannie 136 pounds since last summer. I had a small mess of sweet potatoes yesterday we give a dollar for a small skillet full. I do earnestly hope you and the children are doing well. give my respects to all the connection. I'll close for to day goodby dear I am your Constant husband.

Still at Fredericksburg, VA
March 9th, 1863
…Susan the camp meeting is still going on I went yesterday and heard a verry good surmon. there is nothing but in difference to hinder me from going every day or night at least I know you will think that I ought not to be so in different about preaching. if so, for give me and to God to remember me in his mercies, and to be my shield both against the Yanks and the devil and to give me courage to face the enemy of my Country and God.

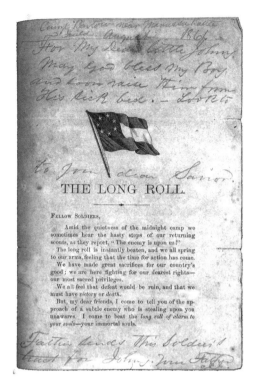

Religious pamphlet owned by the
Reverend John Jones, chaplain of the
8th Georgia Regiment. *Courtesy of the
University of Georgia Libraries.*

Fredericksburg, VA
March the 16th, 1863
*…Susan the camp meeting is still going. Susan I saw something yesterday that
might be termed a sight, as cold as the water was. I stood and saw one preacher
baptize 21 soldiers in the name of the father the Son and the holy ghost. those
were Baptist about ____ were baptized and great many more were sprinkled.*

Fredericksburg, VA
March the 20th, 1863
*…I told you that I saw 21 persons baptized on Sunday before yesterday I saw
13 more baptized. Martin and Willis Crump, Joe Trussel and Tip Wooton
was among the number who was baptized. Martin and Willis was baptized
on yesterday the 19th day of March in the Fredericksburg Canal by the rev.
Mr. Carrel of ala Susan I have been trying religion myself in my own way I
find that want do. So I commenced another way. I went to the mournners seat
night before and last night for the first time in my life. I trust that I will find the
Saviour after a while pray for myself and your own self with all your power.*
John McDonald

Recollections from Captain Wilson T. Jenkins of the 14th North Carolina Infantry:

Battle of Fredericksburg.
Camp near Rappahannock.

After the survival of the army at Fredericksburg, early in the fall of 1862, the 14th Regiment was sent down the river some distance below the city on guard duty. The weather was extremely cold, and the men poorly clad and shod, suffered much. Having nothing to do but picket duty, some of them amused themselves by wading or swimming the river and exchanging tobacco and other things for sugar and coffee, which was very sparse in the Confederate camp. Others fished in the river and swamps to supply their wants for meat.

On the 12th of December, the Regiment had orders to move in the direction of Fredericksburg, as the Federals, under General Burnside were crossing the river for a general advance on Richmond. Early on the 13th, the brigade, commanded by General Ramseur moved by way of Hamilton's Crossing, and into position in line of battle just in rear of front line, supporting a battery commanded by gallant Maj. Pelham. As men were very much exposed to the heavy firing of shot and shell directed at the battery, Gen. Jackson ordered Col. Bennett to put his men out of danger. Accordingly a portion of the regiment, including Company A, was detached and sent to the right to re-establish a line that had been broken by the enemy, and they remained on the firing line until night. General Burnside finding that he had been defeated, escaped to the river and was then relieved of his command.

After the battle of Fredericksburg, the regiment went into camp on the Rappahannock, where they prepared winter quarters and did picket duty until spring. Camp life was cold, dreary and monotonous, with but few furloughs and permits. One member of Company A, (Major N.E. Jenkins) was allowed to spend Christmas in Richmond. During the winter and early spring, the Chaplains of the Brigade, (W.C. Power, A.D. Betts, Col. Osborn and other) commenced revival services, which resulted in the conversion of many of the officers and men, and these spread to other commands until there were great revivals in all or camps. The old songs of Zion could be heard in every company, and many nights after "taps" when the order was that all should be quiet, some happy one would commence singing in low, melodious tones, "When I can read my title clear," or "How firm a foundation," then others would gather, and they would have a regular old camp meeting.

Campfire Cooking

Campaign Diets and Not-So-Fine Dining

The men craved green food, especially after weeks of salt bacon, and would gather and eat rabbit grass.
—Robert Wallace Shand, Company C, 2nd South Carolina Volunteer Infantry, CSA

Despite being absolutely necessary for survival, food for a Confederate soldier was very unreliable fare. Whether marching on campaign or hunkered down in winter quarters, Johnny Reb's dining habits were often dictated by what he could forage or steal from the surrounding area. The Southern army had a commissary department that issued rations, but they were also dependent on the army's ability to maintain the supply lines and keep food from spoiling. Each soldier was typically issued a sparse menu of staples including meat, coffee, sugar and a hard biscuit called hardtack. Confederate soldiers had something called "Johnnie Cake" that they made in the field from cornmeal, milk and a few other ingredients. Their meat would likely be salted or dried into a jerkylike state in order to preserve it as long as possible. Fruits and vegetables were rarities, even in the agricultural South, as the crops in fields and farms were often destroyed or picked clean.

Soldiers on both sides of the Civil War had a different mix of supplies. A Union soldier's haversack would have been filled with salt pork, fresh or salted beef, coffee, sugar, salt, vinegar, dried fruit and vegetables. And if it was in season, they might have fresh carrots, onions, turnips and potatoes. The Confederate soldier typically had bacon, cornmeal, tea, sugar, molasses

Cooks posing at a camp field kitchen. *Courtesy of the Library of Congress.*

and the very occasional fresh vegetable. Southern soldiers were able to trade tobacco, a highly prized commodity, for some of the North's delicacies. Both sides would also commandeer food stores and cooking materials whenever possible from both civilian supporters and reluctant dissidents. Sometimes payment would be offered.

As the war dragged on, the quantity and quality of the food for the Southern forces was dismal. Much like the Continental army during the American Revolution, state governments in the South were supposed to supply their respective soldiers, rather than the central government of the Confederate States of America. This led to a vast inconsistency and lack of organization throughout the army. By 1863, Confederate commanders often spent as much time and effort searching for food for their men as they did in planning strategy and tactics.

Provisions were usually issued uncooked, so the soldiers were required to prepare them according to their own tastes and ingenuity. Small groups would form and combine their measures to prepare a larger and more complex meal. Sharing in the cost and preparation, these bands formed a "mess" and participating members were called "messmates." Some of the more affluent Confederates brought their own personal servants into the field who acted as cooks for the mess. In doing so, they would usually be required to pay out of their own pockets for their slave's portion of the food.

Soldiers in the field were not the only ones suffering from a lack of food during the war years. Civilians in the South also experienced a tremendous decline in their diet. This was due to the fact that the majority of fighting took place in the Southern states, where natural resources would be gobbled up by occupying armies on both sides. Due to a lack of available foodstuffs, the price of provisions soared. Before secession, a typical Southern family's grocery bill was $6.65 per month. By 1864, it was $400 per month. Eventually, Confederate dollars were so devalued that many residents could not afford to buy food staples. And as produce became more and more scarce, people had to find substitutes for common foods. This included some dishes that were obviously formed out of desperation, including domestic animals, crows, frogs, locusts, snails and snakes.

Oliver J. Lehman of 33rd North Carolina Infantry recollected:

> *Rations were usually issued every evening. A supply for the next 24 hours was given out; the amount being about 1 lb flour, ½ lb beef, or in place of beef, ½ lb bacon. One person drew for his company according to the number of his men & he in turn divided it among the mess'es, which were generally 4 to 8 persons. Our camp was counted at 13 men. These rations for 13 men were cut into 13 parts and placed on the ground. One of our number was blindfolded or turned away so he could not see, & another said who gets this? The answer came, Johnny Jones, which he picked up then another said who gets this? until the entire lot is disposed of. No partiality given & everybody satisfied.*

Letter from Spencer Glasgow Welch, a surgeon in the 13th South Carolina Volunteer Infantry (McGowan's Brigade), to his wife:

> *Camp on Rappahannock River*
> *Spottsylvania County Va*
> *December 28 1862*

> *The weather during Christmas has been as warm and pleasant as I ever saw it at the same season in South Carolina, but this morning it was quite clear and cold I like the cold weather here for we have such fine health. It is seldom*

Confederate soldiers dining with what appears to be a cook or body servant. *Courtesy of the National Institute of American History and Democracy.*

that we have a man to die now. Our army was in better fighting trim at the battle of Fredericksburg than at any time since the war began, and it is still in the same condition. It does not seem possible to defeat this army now with General Lee at its head. The Yankees are certainly very tired of this war. All the prisoners I have talked with express themselves as completely worn out and disgusted with it. Our regiment was on picket at the river a few days ago and the Yankee pickets were on the opposite bank. There is no firing between pickets now. It is forbidden in both armies. The men do not even have their guns loaded. The two sides talk familiarly with each other and the Yankees say they are very anxious to have peace and get home. Edwin and James Allen dined with me yesterday and said it was the best meal they had partaken of since they left home. We had fried tripe, chicken and dumplings, shortened biscuits, tea, which was sweetened and peach pie. Ed slept with me and took breakfast with me this morning. He thought my quarters very good for camp. I have a pocketful of money now and while there is a dollar of it left you can have all you wish. I would certainly like so very much to be with you, but it will never do for our country to be sacrificed in order that our selfish desires for comfort and ease may be gratified. It is everyone's duty to lend a helping hand to his country and never abandon his post of duty because a few who have no patriotism do so. While I write I hear Chaplain Beauschelle preaching at a tremendous rate. He seems to think everyone is very deaf I should prefer to hear some ludicrous old negro preacher for that would afford me some amusement. To save my life I cannot think of anything more to write so good by my dear wife. Take good care of George.

Recollections of Robert Wallace Shand, Company C, 2nd South Carolina Volunteer Infantry:

The first year we had plenty of rations, including fine beef. The next year we did not fare so well, and sickened on beef until a change was made to bacon, and then got tired of bacon. Vegetables were as scarce as hen's teeth. The men craved green food, especially after weeks of salt bacon, and would gather and eat rabbit grass and even Irish potatoe tops. A turnip patch was sure to be cooked whenever seen. We had no coffee after 1861, and sugar was very scarce. For the latter we substituted sorghum and for coffee, all sorts of things—dried sweet potatoes, grist etc. parched and sometimes chicory. When on marches, away from our base of supplies, we were sometimes reduced to apples and roasting ears, and sometimes we had nothing but parched corn and water. Therefore we were often hungry.

Recollections of John W. Hamil, Company E, 9th Georgia Infantry:

While we were in Camps, near Fredericksburg in December 1862, there was a citizen who came into our Camps with a two horse wagon load of cakes to sell to the Soldiers. They were sweet; made out of syrup and flour and other things. Now in Va. They bake nearly all their bread in Bakeries. Bakeries are built something like three feet and a half wide and eight or nine feet long. The old man had his cakes about 3½ by 8 feet and squared off about six inches. The sheets of cakes just about fitted into his wagon body. Well, he drove into Camp with about a good two horse load of cakes and his cakes were in demand and very salable at a dollar a piece. The Soldiers crowded around for forty or fifty yards. He began to hand out cake and take in the dollars. He could not wait on them near fast enough. Soldiers were so thick they climbed over each other and he couldn't begin to hand out fast enough. There was a Jew in our Company (a boy like) and he got up on the wagon and both of them handed out cakes and took in the money. Well the rush was so great that neither of them had time to give you your change back, could do that later; you give a dollar you hand in a five dollar bill you got cake. That was not giving satisfaction so some of the boys that was in the right place took out the hind gate of the wagon body; others took off the hind wheels and other give the horses a start and the further they went the faster the horses run. They ran away, tore the wagon to pieces and scattered his cakes as long as there was any to scatter. The Jew had both pockets full of money and in the rush the Jew he forgot to give the old gentleman his money. Well the old fellow that had the cakes had but one remedy: he could go to General Anderson and he would do that so he would and he went to the General and made a complaint, made it as full as he could. General Anderson said to him, "Point out the men." Of course he didn't know any of them so he says to the General, "It's your whole Brigade, Sir." "Well," says Anderson, "if I was to arrest the whole Brigade I would not have a single man to guard them." So the old man was with out a remedy. He went away sadder and a wiser man. His loses were heavy, his experience great.

Letter simply signed "Potomac," a South Carolina infantryman:

Camp 7th S.C. Reg't
Near Waller's Tavern, VA
Sunday, 30th August, 1863

Dear Wilson,

…I have to confess that we have not been supplied with anything like full rations for some time – and during the past two weeks course corn meal has been issued instead of flour, and the troops perfectly abhor the stuff, but we are soldiers and those in authority think anything is good enough for us. It does seem strange that such a thing should exist, while thousands of barrels of good flour is stored away in Richmond (where it will remain until it is partly spoiled) and the Government possessing sufficient transportation to send it forward. We are willing to suffer hardships, and undergo privations, whenever

Members of the 9th Mississippi Infantry share a campfire meal. *Courtesy of the Library of Congress.*

it is necessary; but the idea of suffering—without a cause is more than we bargained for; and it is to be hoped that some one will enquire into the matter. Gen. McLaws has established market expressly for his _____ but soldiers getting only eleven dollars per month cannot afford to deal in the vegetable line very extensively while the planters are permitted to charge ten dollars per bushes for potatoes, and other things in proportion. Green corn is quite abundant in the country and we are professed hands in the "Grab game," I don't think we will perish yet awhile; therefore, our friends at home need not be uneasy about us in that respect...Yours Truly, Potomac

COLORED "CONFEDERATES"

Black Cooks, Body Servants and Slaves

Bill is as well pleased as any Negro you ever saw, he has been to three negro Balls since we arrived at these camps, but he would go off without first asking permission.
—W. Johnson J. Webb, Company I, 51ˢᵗ Georgia Volunteer Infantry.

Throughout the course of the war, Confederate officers routinely brought their slaves with them to act as camp servants and mess cooks. This was done as both a reflection of the officers' social status and for the domestic services provided by the slaves. In some cases, these African Americans would be issued uniforms, and their typical responsibilities included cooking, washing clothes and cleaning quarters. In addition, those slaves with a musical talent were often called upon to sing, dance and play tunes to entertain their masters' staff or messmates. The sincere nature of these relationships is required to be judged on an individual basis, but it is fair to say that the overwhelming majority of blacks in Confederate camps were most likely acting in the role of servants rather than soldiers.

One of these rare individuals who is said to have served in both capacities was Levi Miller. Born in Rockbridge County, Miller accompanied his master into the field as a body servant and was later called upon to nurse him back to health following a serious wounding at the Battle of the Wilderness. Following his master's recovery, Miller is said to have been voted into the regiment as a full-fledged member. He is then said to have fought in multiple engagements, with the most notable occurring at the bloody Battle of Spotsylvania Courthouse.

According to an account by Captain J.E. Anderson, Miller served with courage and honor. He wrote, "About 4 p.m., the enemy made a rushing charge. Levi Miller stood by my side—and man never fought harder and better than he did—and when the enemy tried to cross our little breastworks and we clubbed and bayoneted them off, no one used his bayonet with more skill, and affect than Levi Miller." Following the South's surrender, Miller received a pension from the State of Virginia as a veteran.

An article printed in the Fredericksburg papers stated that one of the longest surviving Confederate body servants was a local man named Cornelius S. Lucas. In captivity, Lucas had belonged to William Pollock of Stafford County, who served in Company H, 47th Regiment, Virginia Infantry. Upon receiving his freedom, Lucas became a minister and eventually operated a coffeehouse and store in the downtown district. It is believed that he too received a pension for his time with the army, as well as a certificate of appreciation from the local United Daughters of the Confederacy chapter.

Some blacks served the entire war in a loyal capacity to their owners, while others escaped the binds of slavery to find freedom across the Union lines. When the Federal army occupied an area, local slaves would use that opportunity to seek refuge among them, some even acting in the capacity of teamsters or stretcher-bearers. Others would enlist as soldiers and return to fight as members of the U.S. Colored Troops. One Fredericksburg widow named Jane Beale commented in her diary on May 12, 1862, about the mass exodus of blacks toward the Northern army. She wrote, "The enemy has interfered with our labour by inducing our servants to leave us and many families are left without the help they have been accustomed to in their domestic arrangements. They tell the servants not to leave, but to demand wages."

Regardless of their roles, or personal motives and loyalties, African Americans on both sides of the conflict served with the same courage and distinction as their white counterparts, whether acting in the capacity of soldier, servant or slave.

Letter from John McDonald of the 13th Mississippi Infantry to his wife:

Camp near Fredericksburg
March 30th, 1863

Well Susan I will resume the writing of my letter by telling you that yesterday and to day is verry cold ice is a quarter of an inch thick this morning I told

Four slaves prepare a kettle meal near Confederate artillerymen. *Courtesy of the Library of Congress.*

you last night what I have done before I begun my letter so I will tell you what I have done this morning. the first thing you know is to get out of bed. the next I brought a bucket of water and wash my face and hands and then folds up the blankets while the other boys cooked a little breakfast and then we joined in and washed our clothes this may surprise you so I will tell you something about it. You see when Rose Williams came back he brought some of his friends with him to go in the same mess. and that made the mess too large so I and Martin Willis Jo Walters and Adam Ulmer seceded from the old mess and the negro that had been doing our washing belonged to Rose, of course the negro then would go with the other mess so we thought that we could gain by doing our own washing rather than to pay 25 cents a garment which would cost me about 75 cents a week enough of this stuff Susan we are still at Fredericksburg tomorrow is the last day of March. I don't see any sign of the buds of trees puting out yet and neither do I see any signs of peace the Yankees are still in sight across the Rappahanoch River...

John McDonald

Recollections of Robert Wallace Shand, Company C, 2nd South Carolina Volunteer Infantry:

John Clarkson of our mess had a negro man named Mander who cooked for us and served our mess. We chipped in and got a horse and wagon and foraging was easy, for the county around was rich in food stuffs. The beef was magnificent drawn largely from Loudon County, which was a garden spot. Chickens, ducks, butter, eggs, buttermilk etc were easily obtained and we fared sumptuously every day. Meantime, we went diligently thro' all the routine of Camp-life. Reveille beat at dawn of day which comes sooner there than in Columbia in June—and later in December. After roll call the boys proceeded to cook their breakfast, but as our mess had a servant we went to sleep again. After breakfast was guard mounting, then company drill, recreation, cooking, dinner, battalion drill, dress parade, cooking, supper, tattoo, sleep. I may here note that on marches and while under arms expecting a fight, a few were detailed to cook for all, and sometimes it happened that there was no cooking at all because there was nothing to be cooked. Guard was divided into three squads, each (called a relief) was on two hours and off four but when off were kept at the guard tent. Details were sent up every day from the ten companies. Each relief had a corporal, and for the whole there was one sergeant, and a lieutenant who was officer of the guard. Each captain in turn was officer of the day. I do not remember how long it was between the times that my turn came. It probably varied on account of absences, sickness and extra duty men. I remember that one night the countersign was "Austerlitz." I told the corporal that our illiterate men would not remember that word. Sure enough the sentinels kept it lively that night. "Corporal of the guard post #3" and "corporal of the guard post #8" etc., and the call was to ask the corporal to tell them again what the countersign was.

On 18 November we again took up our march and covered a distance of 13 miles which took us across the Rapidan at Raccoon Ford on the road to Fredericksburg. The regiment camped the next night at Chancellorsville and on the evening of the 20th went into camp two miles out of Fredericksburg. But on 19th I broke down, and keeping Edwards with me, lost our way, stayed all night with a Mrs. Mason, and reached Chancellorsville in a heavy rain on the afternoon of the 20th. where we stopped, and spent the night in the large house of Mr. Chancellor. After supper two soldiers asked for sleeping quarters. Mr. C. said his house was full and therefore he was sorry that he could give them no place except the loft of his stable. He went out to show them the way, and we wondered whether we would have to take the wagon shed, but when we made the same request of him on his return, he said he could give us a matress on the floor of the dining room. And there we slept comfortably all night. The next evening we rejoined our company in camp.

During all the months of my service, what was camp life? I have mentioned guard mounting (p. 32) and our drills (p. 56). At guard mounting (or troupe) every morning, the 2d Sergeant took the sick and ailing ones to the Surgeon at the hospital tent, who diagnosed and prescribed—the latter according to stock on hand. The noncommissioned officers and men had to get their own wood and water, do their own cooking and washing. and keep their guns clean. The officers had servants for these duties. Until after Sharpsburg, old Manders slave to John Clarkson, did most of these duties for us. He also was a good provider. When we stopped, he would go off and come back with chickens etc. for most of which we paid, but sometimes the old fellow (who was too honest to steal) would "impress" them, or, to use his own phrase, "pressed em." But a disagreement broke up our mess and thereafter, Edwards, Bryce and I slept together, did our own cooking, toting etc.

Robert Wallace Shand

Excerpt from Bradford Ripley Alden Scott's memoirs of the Civil War:

Our negroes had been advised by stragglers from Appomattox to quit work as they were then free; but to their credit be it recorded they continued their accustomed duties on our plantation till one of my brothers called them from the field and set them free himself, telling them they might go where they pleased with help of transportation and supplies from us as far as possible, or else they might remain and finish the crop and be paid for their work. About half of them did this while others drifted to towns garrisoned by troops and went to the bad or disappeared from sight and hearing.

Our "head men" Overton (Hollingsworth) and Henry (Harris) moved to Richmond eventually and were prosperous, comfortable, and honored as long

Colored "Confederates"

Left: Studio shot of a Confederate officer and his body servant. *Courtesy of the Library of Congress*.

Below: Members of the 7th Tennessee Cavalry and their slaves. *Tom Farish Collection*.

This contested illustration from *Harper's Weekly* depicts two black Confederate pickets at Fredericksburg in January 1863. *Frank & Mary T. Wood Print Collection.*

as they lived. And our dear old "Mammy" (Charlotte Tenant) was cared for by our family through years of helpless old age till she died and was buried in the servants' burying ground at Belair beside her good old preacher husband "Uncle Charles."

I have always been thankful that I was born "in Ole Virginny befo' de Wah" so as to remember those times.

After living through the greatest half of our country's history as a nation, and seeing the marvelous discoveries and improvements of the last seventy odd years, in all material arts and sciences from the old ox cart and covered wagon, stage coach, and sailing craft, etc., etc., to the modern express train, automobile, air plane, ocean greyhound, dreadnought battleship, submarine, wireless telegraph, radio voice communication around the globe almost—to say nothing of the wonderful developments in agriculture, mechanics, printing, photography, surgery, medicine, chemistry and all the rest, for peace or war, inaugurating changes in laws and civilizations of the world, with our country in the lead of all the rest in wealth and influence for good and only good let us hope.

Still I am free to confess that in my humble opinion, the Civilization of the Old South, notwithstanding crudities and imperfections when, as a rule, every one knew and kept his place, respected himself and neighbors, kept honestly employed and minded his own business, was the happiest, cleanest, noblest and free-est the world ever saw—in spite of its African slavery (the occasion tho' not the object of our Civil War) imposed on us by others, and recognized by Thomas Jefferson and other statesmen as an evil to be legally eliminated as soon as practicable by gradual purchase, emancipation, and deportation of the slaves by the State.

African slavery was beatific bliss and freedom compared to the political slavery of Reconstruction by non-combatant carpetbaggers and scallawags imposed on the South after the war, or to the corporate industrialized economic slavery, antagonism, unrest, and distrust in our whole country now since the World War.

The first abolitionists I ever heard of were Virginia planters like General Washington and members of the Custis, Lewis, Dabney and other families who by will or deed manumitted their slaves and had them comfortably settled in Liberia or elsewhere abroad.

The free negro was looked down on with contempt by the slaves in Virginia and found it hard to live in the country even though allowed to do so. The more slaves a man owned the prouder they were to belong to him. And a planter who mistreated his slaves or allowed it to be done, as some few did, was socially ostracized.

My father, Mr. James McClure Scott, of Stafford and Spottsylvania Co. discharged overseers and used trusted negro foremen on his plantations. He offered to free one of these servants, Overton, once for saving my oldest brother's life at great peril to himself, but Overton declined the favor, expressly preferring to remain as he was.

All honor to the old Southern slaves who could be implicitly trusted to protect their masters' homes and families even in preference to their own—that I could cite several instances of during the Civil War—but none since. And this is a good place to stop.

CRIME AND PUNISHMENT

Executions, Courts-Martial and Humiliations

There is some of the orneriest men here that I ever saw and the most swearing and card playing and fitin [fighting] and drunkenness that I ever saw at any place.
—*new recruit in the* Civil War Society's Encyclopedia of the Civil War

As the war dragged on into its third and fourth years, soldiers on both sides of the conflict began to flee the army in record numbers. Some were traumatized by the horrors they had witnessed, others were shamed by the atrocities they had committed and many more were disenchanted with the inexperienced officers who ultimately hampered their chances at survival. Southern troops were more likely to desert, as their supplies were dwindling at a more rapid rate compared to their Northern counterparts who were better outfitted. According to Dr. James I. Robertson Jr. in *Tenting Tonight*, one in every seven Confederates would eventually desert. As the soldiers fell into a deeper sense of desperation, the futility of their fight and cause became overwhelming at times. One Rebel soldier wrote, "Many of our people at home have become so demoralized that they write to their husbands, sons, and brothers that desertion is now not dishonorable."

In order to curb a mass exodus from spreading throughout the ranks of the Confederate army, officers were forced to make grim examples of those who were apprehended while attempting to abandon their duty. The odds of successfully escaping were said by some to be three to one in favor of the soldier. Those who were caught, however, were dealt with in a swift and deadly manner. Following a court-martial, deserters would often be sentenced to death by firing squad. These public executions were to be carried out in front of the entire camp in an effort to strike fear in the hearts of future would-be fugitives.

Each prisoner would be given an opportunity for prayer with a camp chaplain or priest and then blindfolded and (hopefully) shot dead in the chest by a group of riflemen who usually had one loaded musket and the rest primed with powder in place of projectiles. This was done to help dispel guilt. Many times the prisoner's body would be positioned so as to fall right into a coffin. Sometimes, the lack of marksmanship among the firing squad required additional volleys to finish the job. This made the horrific affair all the more difficult to watch, as the additional suffering of a fellow countryman was unbearable.

Less drastic punishments involved the public humiliation of wearing berating signage, being forced to do hard labor, the branding of the letter "D" for deserter or "C" for coward on the soldier's hand or cheek or simply being drummed out of camp in a reprehensible fashion. In an age when nobility was held in the highest regard, the dishonor one would bring upon himself and his family by running away was usually deterrent enough. However, as the trauma of war destroyed one's optimism, the risk of death and disgrace became less frightening.

Some Confederate officials were concerned about the negative effect of camp executions on what remained of troop morale. Several states instituted a no-punishment clause for soldiers who willfully returned to their ranks. One governor wrote a public affirmation that stated,

Many of you have, doubtless, remained at home after the expiration date of your furloughs, without the intention to desert the cause of your country, and you have failed to return to your Commands for fear of the penalty to which you may be subjected. Many of you have left your Commands without leave, under the mistaken notion that the highest duty required you to provide sustenance and protection to your families. Some have been prompted to leave by one motive and some by others. Very few, I am persuaded, have left with the intent to abandon the cause of the South.

He added, "I am authorized to say that ALL WHO WILL without delay VOLUNTARILY return to their Commands, will receive a lenient and

Illustration from *Harper's Weekly* depicting an execution by firing squad. *Lee Foundation*.

merciful consideration; and that none, who so return within forty days from this date, will have the penalty of death inflicted on them."

Letter from Spencer Glasgow Welch, a surgeon in the 13th South Carolina Volunteer Infantry (McGowan's Brigade), to his wife:

Camp near Rappahannock River Va
March 5, 1863

Edwin Jim Allen and Ben Strother took dinner with me yesterday and I think I gave them a pretty good dinner for camp. We had biscuit, excellent ham, fried potatoes, rice, light bread butter, stewed fruit and sugar. They ate heartily as soldiers always do. Edwin is not suffering from his wound, but on account of it he is privileged to have his baggage hauled. A man was shot near our regiment last Sunday for desertion. It was a very solemn scene. The condemned man was seated on his coffin with his hands tied across his breast. A file of twelve soldiers was brought up to within six feet of him, and at the command, a volley was fired right into his breast. He was hit by but one ball because eleven of the guns were loaded with powder only. This was done so that no man can be certain that he killed him. If he was the thought of it might always be painful to him. I have seen men marched through the camps under guard with boards on their backs, which were labeled "I am a coward," or "I am a thief," or "I am a shirker from battle" and I saw one man tied hand and foot astride the neck of a cannon and exposed to view for sixteen hours. These severe punishments seem necessary to preserve discipline.

Spencer Glasgow Welch

Letter from Simeon David of the 14th North Carolina Infantry to his mother and father:

Camp Gregg near Fredericksburg Va. March 12—1863

My dear parents:

I will avail myself of an opportunity afforded this morning of writing you to inform you of my continued good health and spirits. I left home Feb the 10th Tuesday, and reached Richmond the following Saturday. I stopped over there one week, having some claims collected for the families of deceased soldiers. I reached the regt. on the 21st of Feb. in the best of health, and found our noble company as well. On Sunday the 22nd of February the biggest snow fell that I ever saw, being on an average one foot in depth. It lay on the ground several days, during which the regt. and brigades had some of the finest sport snowballing I ever saw. The weather for the past ten days has been very changeable, though we have had a good deal of good weather. Everything is quiet on both sides of the Rappahannock, except that the Yankees fired a few artillery shots on yesterday morning. We have had no explanation yet. Our regiment is still in winter quarters and would be doing finely if we could get a little beef to eat. The men have eaten beef till they like it so much better than bacon. A beef's liver is a very rare dish. Officers have to pay high now for their commissaries, 40 cts per pound for bacon, 20 cts for beef, 8 cts for flour. The Government is issuing plenty of sugar now, but we have done without until we do not care much about it. General Lee has just detailed a general court-martial for our Brigade, for the trial of commissioned officers and capital offences, of which I am appointed Judge Advocate. The court is to be a permanent one for the trial of offences already committed. Our captain Lister is under arrest, under charges preferred by myself, and will probably be tried by that court. We are all looking with a great deal of anxiety to Charleston and Savannah…

Love to all. Your affectionate son.
S.B. David

The body of an executed deserter lies next to a coffin. *Courtesy of the Library of Congress.*

Account of deserter execution printed in the September 26, 1863 issue of *Harper's Weekly*:

The crime of desertion has been one of the greatest drawbacks to our army. If the men who have deserted their flag had but been present on more than one occasion defeat would have been victory, and victory the destruction of the enemy. It may be therefore fairly asserted that desertion is the greatest crime of the soldier, and no punishment too severe for the offense...Some of these had enlisted, pocketed the bounty, and deserted again and again. The sentence of death being so seldom enforced they considered it a safe game. They all suffered terribly mentally, and as they marched to their own funeral they staggered with mortal agony like a drunken man. Through the corps, ranged in hushed masses on the hill-side, the procession moved to a funeral march, the culprits walking each behind his own coffin. On reaching the grave they were, as usual, seated on their coffins; the priests made short prayers; their eyes were bandaged; and with a precision worthy of praise for its humanity, the orders were given and the volley fired which launched them into eternity. They died instantly, although one sat up nearly a minute after the firing; and there is no doubt that their death has had a very salutary influence on discipline.

SILENT DEATH

Dysentery, Disease and Sickness

*Future years will never know the seething hell and black infernal
background and it is best they should not.*
—*poet Walt Whitman on the misery he witnessed in hospitals and camps*

It has been estimated that over 620,000 men died during the four years
of America's Civil War. Surprisingly, two-thirds of those deaths were due
to rampant disease and dysentery. Therefore, the majority of the soldiers
who did not come home from the battlefield were actually sick, not shot,
when they passed away. The state of medical advancements left much to be
desired at the time, as the technology that was being developed to take lives
far exceeded the technology to save them. Physicians did not understand
the concept of infection and therefore made little effort to prevent it. Proper
antiseptics and methods of implementation were not yet developed, and the
poor conditions of camps and field hospitals made sterility impossible. No
antibiotics were available either, and even the most minor of wounds could
easily become a fatal infection. While the typical soldier was at very high risk
of being shot and killed in combat, he faced an even greater risk of dying
from disease.

Army camps were literally breeding grounds for all kinds of disease, and
both young and old men died by the thousands from measles, smallpox,
pneumonia and malaria. Poor hygiene, the lack of adequate sanitation
facilities, infected drinking water and the proximity of animals helped
to rapidly spread germs. Exposure to the elements made simple illnesses

Military doctor's medical tent used for examinations. *Courtesy of the Library of Congress.*

Wounded soldiers rest at a temporary hospital near Fredericksburg. *Courtesy of the Library of Congress.*

deadly. At the time, a severe case of diarrhea and dehydration could even be fatal. In an effort to prevent these senseless casualties, the armies established sanitary commissions to educate soldiers on ways to maintain a safer living environment.

American poet Walt Whitman often volunteered at Union camps and hospitals, where he assisted medical personnel in nursing the sick and wounded. He later captured the atrocious conditions that soldiers experienced when he penned the words contained in the epigraph to this chapter. It has been said that a soldier would come under the threat of fire infrequently, but he would be in mortal peril every day from the invisible enemies that sprung from the filth of their camps and devoured their ranks from the inside out.

As thousands of soldiers gathered together in tent cities, many of them were exposed to different communicable diseases for the first time. Hundreds immediately fell prey to these viruses. Their city-dwelling compatriots, however, were more likely to be immune to these diseases. Measles was considered one of the worst diagnoses, and this illness quickly made its mark on the Confederate army. One officer, Surgeon L.J. Wilson of the 42nd Mississippi, recalled a major epidemic that broke out in his camp in 1861. He stated that the rampant disease was "something that astonished everyone, even the surgeons." Within three months, 204 men from three different regiments died. Dr. Wilson was left with over 100 more patients who were crammed into an old tobacco warehouse. Within several weeks, a new regiment could lose half its numbers to the germ.

Perhaps the most common ailments to strike the camping soldier during the Civil War were bowel disorders. The affliction of both diarrhea and dysentery was so widespread that it came to be called "the runs," as those suffering from it would often be seen rushing to find a latrine trench. It also became known as the "Virginia Quickstep" or the "Tennessee Trot." That said, the most devastating sickness to hit the Southern forces was typhoid fever, which was commonly referred to as "Camp Fever." It has been estimated that up to one-fourth of all non-combat deaths in the Confederate army were the results of typhoid. During the winter of 1862–63, troops stationed in the Fredericksburg area suffered in misery as the spread of respiratory sickness enveloped the army. One soldier wrote, "It is fearful to wake at night, and to hear the sounds made from men about you. All night long the sounds go up of men coughing, breathing heavy and hoarse with half choked throats, moaning and groaning with acute pain, a great deal of sickness and little help, near or in the future."

Letter from Winter Posey, Company F, 2nd Louisiana Infantry (Vernon Guards), to his sister:

Camp near Fredericksburg, VA
December 23, 1862

Dear Sister Lizzie,
…This leaves me in fine health, although I suffer some from cold. I have not been sick a day this winter. The health of the army is very good. We have had several cases of small pocks in the brigade but none in the Regiment as yet. I understand that it is raging so in Richmond, that they refused to let you take furlough, even to the wounded soldiers. I suppose that they are afraid that they will sanction it. I don't apprehend any changes. I was vaccinated about a month ago. It took very well. If I were to take it, it would go very light with me. There has been a general order for the whole army to be vaccinated, those that have not been. I think nearly all have been. I write a few lines to Mother in reference to the box of sundries she sent me last year. It arrived a week or two ago. Everything in it was so damaged and spoiled we could do nothing with them. I am very sorry for it, but we appreciated them as though they had come all right…

Present my best regards to all my lady friends and accept a due portion yourself.

Your affectionate brother,
Wint

Excerpts of letters from John McDonald of the 13th Mississippi Infantry to his wife:

April the 4th, 1863

Well Susan. Since I begun this letter one of our company has been discharged. David Malone is the man. he lost his left arm at Sharpsburg Maryland, and has just now got his discharg a fine stout young man he is and turned loose to shift for him self with one arm. he is an old acquaintance of min he lives near Marion Station. Susan I have no news to communicate to you the most interesting object to you is that I am still in good health and tolerably well satisfied. Martin and Willis are both in good health this you know is a great blessing though there is geting to be a great deal of sickness in our regiment I

Dr. Oriana Moon pledged her services to the Confederacy. She later aided the wounded from the Battle of Chancellorsville. *Courtesy of the Woman's Missionary Union.*

believe there was 14 of our company reported sick this morning don't let this appall you atall for they report sick a great deal to keep off of duty I don't do that unless I feel verry bad but there is geting to be a great deal of serious sickness in our regiment. Susan I was detailed to day to go out in the woods to cut fire wood and I noticed the trees and shrubry and use no signs of Spring in fact the ground is frozen to day and verry winday. I shall be looking for a letter in a day or two. Susan I expect to send you a wooden finger ring in this letter one that I made of ivy root is a big rough thing but I know if you get it you will appreciate it highly because I made it and sent it to you. Susan I don't know how to interest you I have nothing write about we get the daily papers every day here. but it seems that there is no news in the whole confederacy. I do the best you can and pray god to help you to do. I hope that we will be spared to live together again this is my prayer. I will close with the hope that you will have a good time. now my dear take good care of yourself and when you get so you cant write get some one of the girls to write for you. May God bless you my dear wife good bye.

John McDonald

Recollections of Robert Wallace Shand, Company C, 2nd South Carolina Volunteer Infantry:

Late in December one of our company died in camp, the doctor said of homesickness, pure and simple. In January, 1863, we had some clear weather and some not. We were in Fredericksburg on picket again on 7th. 8th & 9th. Here I saw boats come over three times under flags of truce, bringing ladies, accompanied by officers, who came to get the dead bodies of loved ones killed on 13th December. Our camp continued near town until 10 January, when we moved camp. We started after midday and a steady rain commenced to fall soon after. We tredged along thro' rain and mud until dark when we went into our new quarters in a grove. The ground was wet and it was late before anyone could start a fire, but one being got others soon followed. So in time we got things fixed up and had a comfortable night's rest. This proved to be my last camping ground.

Letter from William W. Sillers of the 30th North Carolina Infantry to his sister:

Camp near Fredericksburg, Va.,
March 22d/63.

My dear Sister:
Your very affectionate letter, of the 12th inst., was received day before yesterday. I can never be sufficiently grateful for your anxious concern about my spiritual welfare. God knows I have need of all your prayers! God's dispensations are wise and merciful; but generally so thickly veiled that it is almost impossible to discern the ends in view…The effects of death are in a great measure owing to its un-commonness. Death was once terrible to me—I mean the sight of dead persons. But familiarity with battle-fields has hardened my feelings very much. Dead men are only less common then live ones. There is hardly a week passes that I do not see newly-made graves filled from the small numbers of our single Brigade. A poor Soldier gets sick, dies, is buried by the road-side or under the spreading branches of some tree in the midst of a field. No tear is shed. His

name is forgotten. This is the last of him. There is a home-circle somewhere broken; somewhere there are tearful eyes and broken hearts. These are not here: are neither seen nor thought of. Oh! most truly and heartily thankful a man should be, if he is allowed to die at home—away from camp and the field of battle! I feel very sensibly, dear Sister, that I am not grateful, as I should be, to God for his preservation of my sinful life. There are very few associations in camp that have a tendency to make a man pious. I do not omit to pray, or rather I do not neglect prayer entirely; but I do not pray as often and as fervently, as I should.

LOVE LETTERS

Sweethearts, Wives and Last Words

My Darling there is nothing on this Earth (except inability) that could hold me away from you and our dear little children save the great cause, which now engages the minds of every Patriot in our country.
—James Griffin, South Carolina Infantry

Among the thousands of letters that were written in camp by soldiers on campaign during the Civil War, perhaps none is as poignant as the ones penned to their sweethearts. These private accounts of battles, camp life and general experiences are among the most intimate and provide readers today with a window into the innermost personal side of the common soldier. Whether writing to their wives or girlfriends (or sometimes both), men on the march were inclined to compose a much sweeter, poetic and more romantic letter for their ladies than they would for those sent to friends and family. There was always the chance that these verses represented a soldier's last words, prior to an untimely death on the battlefield.

The receipt of mail was a most welcome distraction from the enormous boredom of camp life for soldiers who were far from home. Parcels and care packages were also a great morale booster for those who were fortunate enough to receive them from their families. To write letters home, soldiers purchased paper, envelopes, ink and pens from sutlers. Stationery makers printed many styles of patriotic stationery and envelopes with engravings of camp scenes or political humor, and these were quite popular among soldiers. Usually a more regal design was selected for those tender letters intended for one's female companion. In turn, women would sometimes send scented letters and handkerchiefs to remind spouses or loved ones of their fragrances.

As the war dragged on, writing letters became a challenge at times, due to a widespread shortage of paper, stamps and writing utensils. As resources and supplies dwindled across the South, soldiers were forced to improvise in order to send correspondence back home. After a battle, paper and pencils proved to be a valuable commodity that could be confiscated from fallen foes. Paper was also a popular item to be used for bartering by troops from both sides.

It was estimated that about 90 percent of the white Union soldiers and about 80 percent of the Confederate soldiers were literate. Still, the readability of some of the Civil War–era letters that currently exist is questionable, as the standard of rural education in America was not at the level that exists today. The majority of the Southern troops had an education that was equivalent to the fourth-grade level and many could not read or write at all. Some soldiers would ask comrades to pen the written communications for them as they dictated, while others simply spelled words phonetically.

Composing a letter to one's beloved was only half of the process, as it had to reach its destination in order to be read. The North's postal system was assisted throughout the war by the U.S. Sanitary Commission, which operated on a relatively consistent basis. The South was not as fortunate. On June 1, 1861, both postal services officially separated themselves from each other. The date was chosen by the Confederate Post Office Department. For the next four years, the Southern states struggled to maintain a reliable mail system. Following the South's surrender, service gradually returned to the control of the U.S. Postal Service. By November 1866, more than three thousand of the eight thousand post offices in the South were restored to their prewar status.

Letter from King David Richards, Company A, 57th Virginia Infantry (who was later killed on July 3, 1863, at Gettysburg), to his wife:

Camp Near guinea January 4th 1863

Dear wife I seat my self this morning to drop yo afew lins to let yo no that I am well as comon truly hoping when these few lins cums to hand tha may finde yo an the baby both well an harty harriet I have no nuse to right to yo we are hear in the woods we ante got no tents I dont think think we will stay hear all the winter tims is peaseble now we are bilding little huts harriet I am geting mity

A soldier's family accompanying him in camp. *Courtesy of the Library of Congress.*

tired of staing hear we dont get nothing to eat that is fit to eat sutch bread as we eat hear my dog wood not eat I dont no how we have live as long as we have harriet thare is such chat as givening us all furlows I dont no wether tha will or not but I no one thin if tha dont give me one I will take one an cume enney how I cant stayaway from yo and tha baby much longer it dus seam to me like if I could come home and sed yo all I would give (every thing) enney thing in the worlde I am a goin ta wate tel i sed wether tha will givene me enney ferlw or not an if tha dont I will take one and try it enney how harriet I want yo to rite to me an rite how yo are getting on fore all the pleser I ged is to rede a letter from yo and to her that yo are well I havent got but too leters from yo since I got out of the horspttle give my love and bet respects to all my folks. tel mother that brouse is well an harty I must bring my few lins to a close by sainq I remain yo loving husband untell deth from King D. Richards to harriet Richards rite soon harriet I sent yo aring in a letter when this yo sed remember me

King David Richards

Letter from James Griffin, South Carolina Infantry, to his wife:

Head Qrs of the Legion
Camp Bartow, March 17th, 1862

Again I take my seat to write a few lines to my Darling Wife—I miss your dear kind letters very much indeed. I have no complaint to make to you for it. I am well satisfied that you have written me regularly as usual, but the letters haven't yet found me. I am expecting every day to receive a lot of them. Col Hampton telegraphed to Richmond the day after we came that our Post office at present is Fredericksburg. I have no doubt that they will all find us after awhile. I shall expect to get a letter from you in a day or two in answer to the first one I wrote you after my arrival here, as it ought not to take a letter more than three days to come through, I have been here a week nearly and have but once been outside of my own camp. Yesterday being Sunday, and no drills—I went into the town. It is rather a pretty town situated on the bank of the Rappahannock. It has, I think, about six thousand inhabitants. We have in this vicinity a pretty large body of troops I understand about fifteen thousand. My own private opinion is from the little examination I have made of this country, that we cannot hold this place if we remain where we are. The hills on the other side of the river entirely command those on this side. I don't know whether it will be attempted to fight the enemy here, or advance to meet them on the other side, or whether the army will fall back still farther. My opinion is, between you and me—that we will do the latter. But this is only a conjecture of mine and of course don't wish you to mention it. I presume we won't fight them until we get advantage of position…My Darling there is nothing on this Earth (except inability) that could hold me away from you and our dear little children save the great cause, which now engages the minds of every Patriot in our country. I feel My Darling that you will give me credit for it although I know it will be a painful suspense to you. But if God's will, in His mercy spare my life—the time will soon roll around…I will continue to write to you my Darling as often as I can—but be not uneasy if you do not receive my letters regularly—for we may be moved off at any time and then it may be so that I cannot write regularly. You can continue to direct your letters to this place until I direct you otherwise…Good night my love. Your Jimmie.

James Griffin

Brief letter from Isaac Newton Cooper of the 3rd South Carolina Infantry to his loved ones, followed by his subsequent death notification (Cooper was killed in action and buried at Spotsylvania, Virginia, on or about May 16, 1864):

Camp near Fredericksburg
April 18, 1863
To Sister E.F. Cooper (Edney)
Give my respects to Minervy Cooper. Tell Sister Mary they must write to me. They must nor forget me because I am so far away. Give my love to Brother Dave. Be good boys and stop swearing as it is a bad habit.

Lt. I.N. Cooper to
E.F. Cooper
Near Spottsylvania C.H. May (16 or 26), 1864
It becomes my painful duty to inform you that your husband Lt. I.N. Cooper was mortally wounded on the 8th of May near this village it will indeed be painful intelligence to you and his children to learn of your great loss—he was wounded in the head by a bomb shell and has been lying insensible ever since. The Surgeon thinks he will die in a few hours. I was in hopes at first that he would recover & be [illegible] *to you & his country but he is getting worse.* [illegible] *He was a true friend to me and a brave officer and soldier lost one of my best friends and his country a true and gallant officer and your loss is greater than all. He was anxious to live through this war on account of you and his children and he never lay down at night without praying for you and his children. It is* [illegible]. [signature not legible]

Letter written from P.H. Powers to his wife, wishing her a merry Christmas:

Wife Camp Near Fredricksburg
Dec 25th 1862

My Dearest Wife,
I hardly have the heart to wish you a Merry Christmas this beautiful Christmas Morning because I will know merriment is not for you this day but I can and

Illustration from *Harper's Weekly* depicting a southern belle. *Lee Foundation.*

do wish you a happy day and the same to our little dears, who I suppose must be content with very meager gifts and very few sweet things. I thought of them when I first awoke this morning about day. And wondered what you managed to put in their stockings. Memory went back to the many happy Christmas days we have shared together with them. Alas will the good old times ever return again? And you and I with our little ones dwell together in peace? I hope so. I believe so, but the heart sickens with the deferred hope.

A young Confederate private, most likely in his teens. *Jeffrey Brown Collection.*

So I have been Jim's chief cook for a week since his servant left. Not much time was given me this morning for such sad affections, with the responsibilty of a Christmas breakfast on my mind. So I stirred myself from a warm bed [end of sentence deleted]. *A Major Quartermaster to a Captain* [word missing] *but necessity is a hard master. And you know I can do anything. I am a better cook than Steven. I wish you could have been present to witness my sweets and partake of my viandes, Barbecue Rabbit, Beef Hash with Potatoes, hot bread and coffee. If the darkies all learn as I shall be able to* [illegible] *some assistance. We are very comfortable in camp. have good tents, and wood is in abundance to keep off the frost. I have been axcidingly busy for the last week assisting Jim in paying off the troops and really he needed it. He worries at every thing. Allows every* [illegible] *to suffer his equanimity and makes himself* [illegible]. *I wish from my heart he could get out of the Department he is in. Though I see no hope for him.*

He had a letter from Robert yesterday. All well. And nothing new. I have written you several times since I have been here but as yet have not heard from you. Continue to write some of your letters will [end of sentence cropped off]. *I wrote you some account of the great fight. But you wil see from the papers how terribly whipped Burnside was, and what a commotion it has produced in Yankeedom. I think the sky brightens and our chances for peace improve. But still the war may bring on another year, or event to the end of Lincoln's term. It is as warm this morning as June. And every thing bright. If I only was with you for the day at least I would have a happy Christmas. We are invited to dine with Tom Bullard. And I am* [illegible]. *I must now stop. With love to all.*

Very Affectionately Yours
P.H. Powers

Letter from Milo Grow, Company D, 51st Georgia Regiment (Miller Guards), to his wife:

Nov. 25, 1862
My Dear Wife,
…On the 25th day of November 1862, we are encamped on the Rappahannock River within a mile of Fredericksburgh Va., in a valley or ravine in which we are surrounded by a thicket of small oaks and ivy bushes with a small rivulet running at the bottom. The ravine is one of the many such among the pleasant hills which line the beautiful valley of the Rappahannock on each side.

On the hill tops we can see the enemy encamped on the range of hills beyond the valley with the smoke of their camp fires overtopping the trees for miles on our right and left. Their batteries are visible over the river about a mile and a half away with their guns yawning at us waiting to belch their thunders forth.

Between us lies the beautiful and cultivated valley of the Rappahannock, which takes its course towards the southeast. The river enlivens a scene of rich cultivation and beautiful residences which contrast strangely with the rough and stern aspect of the hostility which surrounds them. On the left towards the west lies the pleasant city of Fredericksburgh, about a mile away. A city of about 16,000 inhabitants, most of whom have now left to avoid the fearful terrors of a bombardment which is now imminently threatened.

Three towering spires are visible and a large expanse of residences, fruit trees, and so forth. The streets cannot be seen from here. The scene from the hill one hundred yards in front of our camp is one pleasure, but like John Bunyan's Grim Monster which haunts his path when in full view of the gates of the Celestial City stand the waving flags and gleaming tents and flickering camp fires of the enemy, with their rattling artillery and almost endless trains of wagons casting gloom upon the scene and filling the mind with stern realities, rather than imaginative pleasures.

Our camp at nightfall is a busy place, echoing with the fall of axes and the hum of men bringing their wood for their night fire in preparation against damps and colds. The nights are cold and often our blankets are covered at dawn with frost as we lie around our fires. We have no tents and our couch is the bare face of mother earth with perhaps a blanket spread upon it.

At night innumerable fires blaze in every direction, our camp fires, around each of which from 7 to 10 men are gathered, cooking their evening repast of fresh beef and flour bread, and then darkling forms in the glimmering light give an air of ghostly life to our ravine. In a long line in each direction our camp fires appear as an offset to the long row of fires beyond the river. Later in the night our ravine seems to be a forest of smoldering fires surrounded by bundles of inanimate life as we lie wrapped in our blankets around them. Here and there stands one by a blaze to warm and drive away the damps and chill of earth and air.

So the dawn finds us…
Devoted Milo

On the Homefront

Civilian Memoirs and Experiences

My sisters were very nice to these defenders of our country, and played on the piano and sang for them, and they taught my sisters to play cards, which my mother disapproved.
—Mrs. Sue Chancellor, resident of Spotsylvania County, Virginia

Soldiers were not the only ones who were forced to endure hardships during the Civil War. As the conflict was literally fought in the streets of towns and the fields of farms, local civilians experienced the harsh realities of war close up and personal. Whether sacrificing their own privacy and comfort for friendly soldiers in need of rest and reprieve or rationing their food and crops to feed the hungry, residents of an area occupied by an army were often called upon to assist whether they liked to or not.

Following a battle, enemy forces would often commandeer private dwellings for use as headquarters, field hospitals or even a stable. Often, civilian supplies and necessities were raided by foragers. In the South, wealthier plantation owners would periodically host armies on their land for winter quarters, and many of them would later lose their properties either by wartime damage or peacetime foreclosure. Some registered their own observations and experiences with the army in their diaries and memoirs. According to the Fredericksburg/Spotsylvania Military Park Service:

An often overlooked aspect of the Civil War is its impact on the civilian populace of North and South. Fredericksburg, Virginia, for example, was

occupied on three separate occasions by Union forces. These "invasions" of the town had a distinct psychological impact on the townspeople. Through the Civil War era writings of Fredericksburg residents it is possible for us to experience some of their anxiety and fear toward the Union army and also the elation of Confederate success.

Historians today are grateful for the memoirs that were penned by those who were innocent observers caught up in the conflict. Their keen and unbiased observations were sometimes more accurate than the official military reports that were filed with the Federal and Confederate governments. And their suffering was also evident, as the battles of this particular conflict took place right in their own backyards. The residual destruction following a skirmish manifested itself in ruined buildings and scarred landscapes that proved devastating to the South's economy and infrastructure. Additionally, the mere presence of an army encampment ravaged the nearby communities by depleting their crops, poisoning their water supply, commandeering their livestock and damaging their roads.

Following a major engagement, the U.S. Sanitary and/or Christian Commission, a Protestant charity organization, would arrive in town, tasked with assisting the remaining inhabitants in dealing with the thousands of bodies and potential sicknesses that could result from rotting corpses. Members of the organization would also help to render aid to the wounded soldiers who were left behind in makeshift field hospitals and churches. These were the men who were wounded badly and could not move during an army's redeployment or retreat. More often than not, they were left to the mercy of local doctors and volunteers. Regardless of what side of the conflict retained their loyalties, most civilians during the Civil War preferred not to see an army anywhere near their homesteads.

Excerpts from the diary of Sue Chancellor, as compiled by Emily W. Fleming:

My first recollection of the war is about the Confederate pickets. They used to be stationed near us and come in and get their meals from my mother. We had plenty of servants then and my mother was a good provider, so they thought

Opposite, top: Refugees fleeing a war-torn area with a wagonload of possessions. *Courtesy of the Library of Congress.*

Opposite, bottom: Daguerreotype of Citadel cadet George McDowell (class of 1862) with his younger siblings. *Courtesy of Tyler & Co., South Carolina.*

themselves in clover. My sisters were very nice to these defenders of our country, and played on the piano and sang for them, and they taught my sisters to play cards, which my mother disapproved, but they all seemed to have a good time. They were mighty nice to me, too. I remember one Sunday a drove of sheep coming down the road, and one of them said: "Sue, wouldn't you like to have a pet?" I, of course, was delighted, and he went out and bought me a beautiful white lamb. His name was Thomas Lamar Stark, from Columbia, S.C., and I named the lamb "Lamar" and kept it until the house was burned. When the Confederates went away and the Yankees came, I brought the lamb into the house every night to keep it from being killed.

Excerpts from Bradford Ripley Alden Scott's memoir of the Civil War:

They told us of a famous young violinist they had in their command named Carlo Patti, brother of Adelina Patti, just then coming into fame as a songbird. One evening after our soldier guests had recovered and returned to camp we were treated to a serenade by their talented young comrade. I say "we," for though this music was close enough to the house I was the only one who heard its soft strains, being already wakeful from pain of a blinded eye. The hour was late, but it did not occur to me that the others needed to be awakened, till next morning and afterwards when I was berated for neglecting them when they learned what they had missed. I have repeatedly since been awakened by entrancing music, but never heard anything to equal the soft expressive soul talk of that violin.

We spent the night in the camp of this Co. "G," 9th Ala. infantry further down the road near Fredericksburg and heard their account of the Salem Church fight. One young fellow from the piney woods who probably never owned a negro and never expected or cared to own one, like many others in the Southern army, but was none the less a venomous states' rights "Reb," was being joked by his companions around the supper fire that evening about his noticeable rapid and deadly aim out of one of the Salem church windows, and the number of men seen to fall when he fired. He blushed like a girl and walked off teased and remorseful about it. Less than sixty days afterwards this same boy, with his fighting blood up again, fell dead in helping to capture a battery at Gettysburg, just as he reached a cannon he had pointed out and claimed as his individual prize.

After the Gettysburg campaign, in the summer or fall of 1863, Gen. McLaw's Division of Longstreet's Corps was camped for some weeks near us in the S.W. end of Spottsylvania County, recruiting and resting from their labors, and quite a few of their wounded officers were quartered in nearby plantation residences of friends. I remember helping to wait on one of them, a Major Jones of South Carolina, who had his knee shattered by a minnie ball. He said he preferred to die rather than have his leg amputated and, before long, had that choice about it, we heard with much regret.

Letter from Samuel S. Brooke's sister on the occupation of Fredericksburg:

Fredericksburg, April 17th/62

Dear Sam & Mr. Bruce-
The Yankees will be in town today at eleven o'clock. This may be the last letter I shall be able to write you for some time. The enemy took Falmouth yesterday. Our forces retreated yesterday, and now not a Confederate flag, soldier, or tent can be seen. Our force is said to have been [3,200?], *the Yankees are estimated at from 15,000 to 800* [may have meant 1,500 or 8,000]. *We had some skirmishing with them and lost a man or two, several men wounded, we killed several of the enemy. It was the saddest sight I ever saw, to see our men retreating yesterday, almost at double quick, leaving us behind to the enemy, and the black smoke rolling up from the burning bridges.*

They sent a white flag over yesterday and we sent some men with one back to them. Then two Yankees came over and said, "Gen. Augur (their Gen.) said he would take possession of the city at eleven oclock today and that private property should be respected," but who believes a word they say. We tried to hide every thing we could yesterday. I am afraid Mr. William Moncure is going to leave us. I suppose you know we have Mrs. W. Moncure & family & Mrs. Bankhead with us. We have gotten fixed in our new home and are as comfortable as circumstances admit. Mr. [A____t] *is very kind to us. Yesterday he was here three times—we value a friend now highly.*

A great many people left town yesterday. The trains will only run to [__ lford] *now. The last one went out yesterday. I do wish we was behind the lines and feel much afraid of the Yankees, but I know it was impossible for us to go, and we will have to make the best of it. It all looks very dark now, but I know nothing happens by chance, and whatever is, must be the best for us. I do hope brighter days are coming.*

Excerpts from the diary of Ms. Matilda Hamilton:

Tuesday, 25th Nov. 1862. The Rappahannock is a barrier and safeguard to us. Generals Lee, Jackson, Longstreet are all here. The Army is 40 or 80,000 strong, I hear. Since the 20th, when we have been in the midst of a large army, I could not tell, nor write down the confusion we have been in, nor enumerate the persons we have entertained and had here at Forest Hill. People are moving and countermoving, dying to avoid the Yankees, for scarcely anyone who remained with them last summer was willing to stay again. And then some moved back when they found the town was to be defended. Jack Marye's family and Sister Charlotte's have left Fredericksburg. They are all here vows Milly, her five children, two servants, and Mary Browne, Sister Charlotte, three grand children and two servants. They have all been here since the 21st.

Thursday, 4th Dec. Fergus, Emily and myself walked to Eastern View. As I looked from that eminence and viewed the extensive prospect which stretched before us, I thought how strange the sight. What an upheaval of our once peaceful neighborhood. A brigade here, a regiment there, and tents and soldiers everywhere. We constantly have rumors of battles, of the advance of the enemy, of the expected battle. Burnside, the young Napoleon of the Yankees, has taken the place of McClellan. He is to make the onward march to Richmond. With him is Patrick, who figured in Fredericksburg so favorably last summer. I don't praise any of the Yankees myself.

Thursday, 1st January 1863. We are surrounded by soldiers, and everything gives place to the military. General Lee's army, which has just gained such a world-wide renown from the victorious campaign of '62, lies encamped around us. On the other side of the Rappahannock, not half a mile away, is the Yankee army. This day last year the war was going on, but we had not felt it. But how we have seen war and it is dreadful. I felt uneasy then, but how would our hearts have fainted within us if we could have known what was before us—the dreadful battles, so bloody, so long continued. Virginia ravaged, desolated, her sons slain, her daughters weeping—her soil watered with the blood of her best and bravest. We feel hopeful now, but we know not what the new day may bring forth—then 'tis fearful to think what the year just commenced may have in store for us.

Virginia troops petition Southern sympathizers for food in this painting by Confederate veteran William Sheppard. *Courtesy of the Museum of the Confederacy.*

Sometimes soldiers would be taken in by charitable families. Letter from Jesse McGee:

Camp 7th So Ca
Near Walter's Tavern
Sept 6th 1863

My dear Mollie,
Yours of Aug 30th was rec'd on day before yesterday, & read with usual interest. I was glad to hear of your good health, spirits & c.

Since I last wrote you we've moved about 15 miles to our present camp we are now in Spotsylvania County a convenient distance from the Central R.R. in the best country we've been in since the first year of the war, we can get planty of vegetables fruit, & c, at tolerably reasonable prices, & with what we draw & buy, we are now living pretty well for soldiers, but I fear we will not stay hear long we've been hear two weeks to day (Sunday).

I've formed the acquaintance of a very nice family in this vicinity by the name of Lipscomb (a Widr Lady) where I'm treated like I was at home, the day after we came hear I went out & formed the acquaintance dined with them, & spent a few pleasant hours in conversation with her Daughter of which she has three very nice indeed, & in a few days I recd & invitation to dinner with them again, (it is needless to say I accepted) & I assure you it was a rich treat; for they had nearly evry vegetable that grows in the country on the table, very nicely prepared so you may guess that I did ample justice to the many nice things. I & Mr. Carlisle (the preacher) went over last Wednesday & spent the day very pleasantly with them and partook of another one of their good dinners. Such friends are worth having in the war. If you hear of me marrying or being engaged to one of the young ladies soon, you need not be surprised. I spent yesterday evening very pleasantly with them.

SONS OF SECESSION

Letters to the Family of Life on Campaign

*I know your heart leaped with joy at the inteligence that I was safe I know
that you was filled with gladness and I hope while I continue to battle in
the service of my country.*
—*W. Johnson J. Webb, Company I, 51ˢᵗ Georgia Volunteer Infantry*

Some historians have referred to the American Civil War as "The Boys'
War," as so many young men tragically fought and died in the conflict.
Teenage boys who were filled with delusions of grandeur routinely lied
about their age in order to enlist in the army. Many of these teen soldiers
were exposed early on and relegated to the role of drummer or stretcher-
bearer. Unfortunately, as the war dragged on, more and more recruiting
drives appear to have turned a blind eye to these fraudulent enlistments as
the necessity of replenishing warm bodies in the field became paramount.
Even the young men who were technically of age were woefully innocent.
More often than not, they were away from home for the first time in their
lives. This fact is often painfully apparent in the tone of the letters that
were sent home. Many boys wrote to their mothers to assure them of
their safety, while at the same time expressing a childlike longing for their
families and firesides.

Thousands of teenagers, whether polished military cadets or illiterate
farm boy volunteers, have served as soldiers throughout America's history.
They fought against the British in the American Revolution and against
one another in the Civil War. Each one stood on skirmish lines alongside

men old enough to be their grandfathers, and many fell dead on the same bloody fields as their fathers. For every one of these senseless deaths, a grieving mother was left back on the homefront. During the War Between the States, scores of underage boys served in the ranks of both armies. Many served with distinction, including the cadets of the Virginia Military Institute, who joined in the Battle of New Market in May 1864 to save the fertile Shenandoah Valley. Along with the regular Southern army, they marched eighty miles in four days. Initially, the cadets were to form the reserve, but they were instead used to plug a gap and later charged the enemy. Confederate general Breckinridge rode by, doffed his hat and shouted, "Well done!"

Letter from J.T. McElvany, Company F, 35th Georgia Infantry, to his parents:

Camp in the Woods near Fredericksburg Va. Dec. 19. 1862

My Dear Mother,

I received a letter from you a long time ago and have been promising to write you ever since. I now hasten to redeem that promis, I hardly know how to commence to interest you, To tell you of the dangers through which I have passed through which I am likely to have to pass again would be any thing but pleasant to you. We are camped in the woods about six miles from Fredericksburg. We have no tents and but one Blanket each. The ground is now frozen hard and you can guess what kind of Camp fare we have…We get very good fare when we are stationed but while we were in line of Battle, where we lay four days, we had rough fare. Rob. is a little unwell but not unable for duty. I have a bad cold myself, but I am only surprised that I am not down sick nobody knows what a man can stand untill he, tries it. I have got me a good pair of boots and a new pair of pants I need some shirts socks & hat & drawers. But I see no chance to get them now. I would like to have a new over coat and dress coat too.

…I have about played out, if I have failed to interest you it is not my fault, I have done the best I could. I was glad to see a letter from you, and shall be glad to see another. I will try appreciate the advice you gave me, and comply with your request give my love to all the family and accept the same yourself I will try to be more promt next time in writing let me hear you for I get letters very slow from Home. So many of you ouht to write us once a week at least I must close: I remain your affecionate Son

Sons of Secession

Letter from W. Johnson J. Webb, Company I, 51st Georgia Volunteer Infantry, to his mother:

Camps 51st Ga Regt.
Near Fredericksburg Va
23rd 1863.

Dear Mother.
About five minutes ago I received your letter of the 17th and I assure you that it was a welcomed visitor. for i was anxious to hear from home. not having heard since the fight. I know your heart leaped with joy at the inteligence that I was safe I know that you was filled with gladness and I hope while I continue to battle in the service of my country to ever be abel to give sich joy. After the several engagements through which I have to go You say that you felt all the time that I was safe. And I must say that ever while I was in the battle and the leaden hail and shells playing round and over me as thick as the most expansive imagination could conceive I felt secure from harm. and very much unconcerned about my own person The cause of which I know not (for I am certain there was danger) and I know not even until this day. but I presume that I was saved by prayer not my own but those of others and I hope in that good deed you will meet with a just and happy recompense. Our army will in a few days make a move. whether we go forward or fall back towards Richmond I know not. there are different opinions as to our move Enough of the war and the army for I am tired of both and would like to talk of neither again. I am almost willing to exclaim in the language of Cooper

"Oh; for a lodge in some vast wilderness. Some boundless contiguity of shade Where the rumors of oppression and deceit Of unsuccessful or successful war Might never reach me more!"

but in this there would be no enjoyment for me. for I could not forget that mother and that father who nurtured me from infancy to manhood that brother who was the partaker of all my saddness and joy during his boyhood career Could I ever forget the young ladies of Ft Gaines who's society I was once so much enjoyed? Even the Miss Dorrie Mount, might haunt me at night. upbraid me with the recollection that I had a prior time been "snuffed." Would not this be mortifying to see you suppose? She has certainly forgotten that for the last fourteen months my little Bark has been cast out on a sea who's waves have rolled high and tossed to and for the mighty notions of the earth with none to stere the bow and guide the rudder but myself. [W.J.J. Webb]

Period illustration depicting a campfire minstrel show. *Courtesy of the Fredericksburg/Spotsylvania NMPS.*

Letter from Steven Dandridge of the Rockbridge Artillery to his mother:

Camp near Fredericksburg
December 19th 1862
My Dear Mother
God has mercifully [illegible] *me through another great battle. since I wrote to you last, our company has been terribly cut up. In the battle of Fredericksburg we lost 6 killed, and ten or twelve badly wounded, our camp is nothing like it used to be, a look of sorrow now sits upon the countenance of every one. Ed & Lem both came out of the fight unhurt. Oh! How thankful we ought to be to that God who has mercivully protected us. I think that we have had our last fight for this winter*

Tell Sal that Pelham had command of us in the fight. He said that he would keep us until I got killed and then he would relieve our company. He is as gallant a fellow as I ever saw. Tell Sal that Col. Rossner enquired about her. He too was with us the night of the fight. You must write to me if you can. You don't know how much I want to see you. Goodbye. Give my love to everyone at home, Black and White. I hope you will soon see your son,

Tell Mary [illegible] *that Auther Robinson was shot through the leg. The bone was not broken though the ball went through it.*

Letter from Michael F. Rinker, Company F, 136th Virginia Militia, to his parents:

Camp Near Spotsylvania Court-House Va
Tuesday May the 17th 1864
Dear Father and Mother
With pleasure I write to you this morning, hoping you may get this in due time. I am well, and hope you are all well. I must ask you to excuse me for not writing sooner, indeed I am ashamed that I have not written ere this. But now I will tell you why I did not write to you sooner than I did.

We have been so busy since we came over here, that indeed this is the first chance that I have had to write. The second day after we arrived here, we commenced fighting and it is not over yet. Father indeed for 5 days we were so busy fighting that we could hardly get time enough to eat our meals. To-day it is 14 days since we commenced fighting and yesterday the cannon and small arms were still at work. But the fight was not real heavy all the time, the hardest fighting was on the 5.6.& 7 and on the 9, 10 & 11 days of this month. During them six days it was awful. There was one continual roar of thunder all the time from the artillery and small arms.

For six days the Battle was kept up, all the time day and night, in the dead hour of midnight, the cannon & musketry was thundering all the time. Column after column the Yankees pushed their men up to our Breastworks and our men were cutting them down as fast as flies. The dead Yankees are heaped up in piles half as high as a man, in front of our Breastworks, and all around on the Battlefield the dead yanks are lying just as thick as they can be, and none of them buried, they will all rotten on top of the ground.

Now you may know how it is down here. The line of Battle is 15 miles long, and for 4 days the Battle was kept up all along the line. The Yankee loss in killed and wounded is awful. Their loss will not fall short of fifty five hundred in killed and wounded, and their loss in prisoners, will reach ten or twelve thousand. We have captured 12 or 15 fine pieces of artillery and 6 or 8 thousand small arms. The yanks lost in killed, 2 Major Generals and 3 or 4 Brigadier Generals, and their loss of Officers generally in killed wounded & prisoners is large. Their entire loss is very heavy, and I think it will be larger yet, before the fight is ended.

All the men say that this has been the hardest fight, since the war. It was awful for about 5 days, the cannon just kept one continual roar of thunder, day and night. I suppose you have heard, of the number of killed and wounded, of our company. You have also, no doubt heard that General J.E.B. Stuart died a few days ago from a wound received near Hanover Junction. General Longstreet was painfully wounded on the second day of Battle. But he is getting well fast.

General Lee got a dispatch yesterday afternoon from General Breckinridge stating that he had whipped and routed the yanks 2 miles above New Market and run them to Mt. Jackson where the yanks burnt a Bridge. We are all glad to hear, that the yanks have been whipped in the valley. Noah is well. We have plenty to eat. Noah give me the things that you sent to me and I am very much obliged to you for them. I will try and bring something when I get home. Tell mother, I would like to have one pair of socks sent to me by the first one of our men that comes over. Write soon and give me all the news. I hope you will excuse me for not writing sooner, for indeed I did not have time hardly to eat my meals, we were busy all the time. I will close. Your son. Michael F. Rinker.

Our men are still in line of Battle, day & night all the time, some times they commence fighting at midnight. There is no telling how much longer the fight will last. Our men lay in our Breastworks day and night. One night last week the yanks charged our Breastworks 9 different times, and every time our men run them back, with great slaughter. If I can get time I will write to you soon or as soon as I hear from you all. I will close.
Your son, Mike.

Letter from Tally Simpson to his sister:

From: Tally Simpson
To: Anna Simpson

Camp near Fred'burg
Dec. 25th

My dear sister,
This is Christmas Day. The sun shines feebly through a thin cloud, the air is mild and pleasant, [and] a gentle breeze is making music through the leaves of the lofty pines that stand near our bivouac. All is quiet and still, and that very stillness recalls some sad and painful thoughts. This day, one year ago, how many thousand families, gay and joyous, celebrating Merry Christmas, drinking health to absent members of their family, and sending upon the wings of love and affection long, deep, and sincere wishes for their safe return to the loving ones at home, but today are clad in the deepest mourning in memory to some lost and loved member of their circle.

Federal troops ransack a Confederate winter camp. *Courtesy of the Fredericksburg/Spotsylvania NMPS.*

If all the dead (those killed since the war began) could be heaped in one pile and all the wounded be gathered together in one group, the pale faces of the dead and the graons of the wounded would send such a thrill of horror through the hearts of the originators of this war that their very souls would rack with such pain that they would prefer being dead and in torment than to stand before God with such terrible crimes blackening their characters. Add to this the cries and wailings of the mourners—mothers and fathers weeping for their sons, sisters for their brothers, wives for their husbands, and daughters for their fathers—[and] how deep would be the convictions of their consciences.

Yet they do not seem to think of the affliction and distress they are scattering broadcast over the land. When will this war end? Will another Christmas roll around and find us all wintering in camp? Oh! That peace may soon be restored to our young but dearly beloved country and that we may all meet again in happiness. But enough of these sad thoughts. We went on picket in town a few days ago. The pickets of both armies occupy the same positions now as they did before the battle. Our regt was quartered in the market place while the others occupied stores and private houses. I have often read of sacked and pillaged towns in ancient history, but never, till I saw Fredricksburg, did I fully realize what one was. The houses, especially those on the river, are riddled with shell and ball. The stores have been broken open and deprived of every thing that was worth a shilling. Account books and nots and letters and papers both private and public were taken from their proper places and scattered over the streets and trampled under feet. Private property was ruined. Their soldiers would sleep in the mansions of the wealthy and use the articles and food in the house at their pleasure. Several houses were destroyed by fire. Such a wreck and ruin I never wish to see again. Yet notwithstanding all this, the few citizens who are now in town seem to be cheerful and perfectly resigned. Such true patriots are seldom found. This will ever be a noted place in history.

While we were there, Brig Genl Patrick, U.S.A., with several of his aides-de-camp, came over under flag of truce. Papers were exchanged, and several of our men bought pipes, gloves, &c from the privates who rowed the boat across. They had plenty of liquor and laughed, drank, and conversed with our men as if they had been friends from boyhood. Pres Hix came for the remains of Nap his brother and Johnnie Garlington yesterday and will take them to Richmond today. They will be carried on home immediately. Tell Aunt Caroline Jim is getting on finely. Howdy to all the negros. I have received the bundle of clothes sent to Columbia. The bundle contained one shirt, one scarf, and two pairs of socks. At least I suppose it is the one you sent to Col[umbia] to be sent to Barnwell at Richmond. I am a thousand times obliged. When is Harry coming?

There is nothing new going on. I am almost dead to hear from home. I have received no letters in nearly three weeks, and you can imagine how anxious I am. The mails are very irregular. I hope to get a letter soon. Dunlap Griffin is dead, died in Richmond of wounds received in the last battle. Capt Hance is doing very well. Frank Fleming is in bad condition. (He has been elected lieutenant since he left.) Write to me quick right off. I wish to hear from you badly. Remember me to my friends and relatives, especially the Pickens and Ligons. Hoping to hear from you soon I remain
Your bud
Tally

Excerpts of letters from John McDonald of the 13th Mississippi Infantry to his sister:

In the ruined old city of Fredericksburg, Va.
January the 24th, 1863

Miss Fannie King
Dear Sister...Let me tell you something about our quarters our mess is up stairs in a three story brick house with a splendid fire place there is two rooms on each floor all there is to make us uncomfortable is the nearness of the enemy. Our Brigade I understand will stay here in town all winter or untill the Yankees leave here or drive us out they can make it verry unpleasent for us as they did on the 11th of December, they cant make it much worse in the same length of time. Fannie I have not saw Martin in a week as he was left at camps on guard duty he has not been with the regiment in two weeks I hear from him every day. I am looking for him in town this evening he was well the last time I heard from him he is farther from the Yankees than I am. he is about 3 miles off. Joe Watters enjoys good health we have a few cases of sickness in our company Dick Hoy died of his wound that he got in this battle. I will close by asking you to write soon and give my love and respects to all the family and except a sisters share yourself. I am your brother in love and law.
John McDonald
P.S. Send this to Susan. I recieved a letter from her a few days ago, they were well, be sure to write to me soon.

Letter from A. Howard, a private in the Confederate army (who was later killed at Gettysburg), to his father:

Camp near Fredericksburg
Christmas morning
My dear Father,
I received your letter of the 22nd. [torn] today I was very glad indeed to h[torn] home once more as it was the first [torn] I had heard from home in nearly 4 mon[torn] I was very much releived to hear that all were well at home. I was sorry to hear that Tom was ill all of the time that he was at home. I suppose you will have heard of the great battle of Fredericksburg before this letter reaches you. The Yankees sustained the most utter and terrible defeat, probably that they have experienced during the war. It was the most glorious victory we have ever gained, our loss is trifling in comparison with the enemy,

Above: Typical Confederate army camp in central Virginia. *Courtesy of the Library of Congress.*

Left: Virginia recruiting poster appeals for volunteers to defend their homes and firesides. *Courtesy of the Library of Congress.*

according to Gen. Lee's report of the battle our loss was 1800 killed wounded and missing, while that of the enemy according to their own statement was 15,500, and many of their papers place it as high as 20,000. Not more than one half of our forces were engaged [torn]r brigade did'nt fire a gun. Gen Lee [torn]d that we had suffered so severely [torn] Gaines farm, Manassas No 2 and Sharps[torn]rg, and that he had called upon us so [torn]ften in tight places, that we should be held in reserve. Our regt had 5 or 6 men wounded by shell, no one was killed. I think that we will go into winter quarters soon, as the yankees seem to be disgusted with their ill success of this winters campaign, & they are said to be going back to the Potomac, to go into winter quarters.

The yankee scoundrels almost completely destroyed Fredericksburg, they vented their malice & spleen in the most wanton manner, Breaking up and destroying whatever they could not remove. Nothing was too pure or sacred for their unbridled lust. The very churches were pillaged of whatever of value or ornament they contained. The retribution they received for their iniquitous proceedings was sudden and terrible. The town was literally choked with [torn] dead. There was 5,000 dead bodies of [torn]kee soldiers lying stiffening on that [torn]d field the day after the fight. And [torn]he fight had been general throughout the whole line, the yankee army would have been nearly annihilated, as it was their army was completely demoralized and recrossed the river more like a rabble rout than the grandest army the world ever saw as the yankees were so fond of terming it. The weather for the last few days has been admirable and to day it is as mild and beautiful as any Christmas I ever remember having seen in Texas.

Tell Ma not to be the least uneasy about my personal comfort. I have plenty of good clothes and blankets and have been in excellent health ever since the fall set in.

There is'nt much preparation for Christmas in camp, the boys are in excellent spirits however, not much doing in the egg-nog line, but with butter, molasses, sugar, confederated c[torn] and apples, from the sutler's, and peas [torn] roast-beef and hot biscuit from our own [torn] we managed to make out a pretty good [torn] dinner. I wish I could send some apples, nice red rosy cheeked fellows to Nellie and Susie, bless their little hearts. I am going down to see Conway sometime during the C.X. who is camped about 8 miles below here near Port Royal. I got a letter from Aunt Ellen a few days ago, all were well. I send this letter by private conveyance and will send some papers with it.

Good bye my dear father, God bless and preserve you all from every danger. Give my best love to all, and to Charlie and Tom whenever you write.
your affectionate boy
A Howard

WINTER QUARTERS

Cabins, Markers and Snowball Fights

We are not sorry I assure you for to be exposed [to] such weather as this without fire would be almost death to us.
—*Samuel C. Clyde, 2ⁿᵈ South Carolina Infantry*

In the nineteenth century, armies on both sides of a conflict would often go into a prolonged camp state during the winter months. Due to the inclement weather and cold climate, troops in that period were hampered by the elements and unable to fight, march or transport artillery. Armies would often be stationed on or near the property of a wealthy civilian supporter, and officers would sometimes commandeer outbuildings on the plantation to be used as staff offices and headquarters. Unlike the provisional tent camps that were constructed while on campaign during the warmer months, these winter quarters were far more structurally sound and permanent in their construction.

Most of these shelters were constructed of logs, which would be cut en masse from a local forest area and assembled in a pseudocabin configuration. Soldiers would create a framework for the hut and then stretch canvas or place wooden planks across the top. The quality of the building was solely dependent on an individual's skill and the ability to acquire the necessary materials. Some of these cabins came complete with furniture made from scraps, while others held hammocks or bunk beds. Many times, a crude fireplace was constructed and a chimney, made from mud and rocks, was attached. This kept the cabin dry and warm and allowed the men to cook indoors. Some winter camps even had plank roads running through them, and they took on the appearance of a community with laundries, hospitals and chapels.

Letter from General Robert E. Lee, commander of the Army of Northern Virginia, to his daughter:

CAMP FREDERICKSBURG
February 6, 1863

I read yesterday my precious daughter your letter and grieved very much when last in Richmond at not seeing you. My movements are so uncertain that I cannot be relied on for anything. The only place I am to be found is in camp and I am so cross now that I am not worth seeing anywhere. Here you will have to take me with the three stools the snow the rain and the mud. The storm of the last twenty four hours has added to our stock of all and we are now in a floating condition. But the sun and the wind will carry all off in time and then we shall appreciate our relief. Our horses and mules suffer the most. They have to bear the cold and rain tug through the mud and suffer all the time with hunger. The roads are wretched almost impassable. I heard of Mag lately. One of our scouts brought me a card of Margaret Stuart's with a pair of gauntlets directed to Cousin Robert. I have no news General Hooker is obliged to do something I do not know what it will be. He is playing the Chinese game trying what frightening will do. He runs out his guns starts his wagons and troops up and down the river and creates an excitement generally. Our men look on in wonder give a cheer and all again subsides in statu quo ante bellum. I wish you were here with me to day. You would have to sit by this little stove look out at the rain and keep yourself dry. But here come in all the wet adjutants general with the papers. I must stop and go to work. See how kind God is we have plenty to do in good weather and bad.

Your devoted father
R.E. LEE

Letter from General Robert E. Lee, commander of the Army of Northern Virginia, to his wife:

CAMP FREDERICKSBURG
February 23, 1863

The weather is now very hard upon our poor bush men. This morning the whole country is covered with a mantle of snow fully a foot deep. It was nearly up to

Above: Example of winter cabin structures and camp layout. *Courtesy of the Library of Congress.*

Below: Illustration depicting a snowball battle between Confederate forces. *Courtesy of the Fredericksburg/Spotsylvania NMPS.*

my knees as I stepped out this morning and our poor horses were enveloped. We have dug them out and opened our avenues a little but it will be terrible and the roads impassable. No cars from Richmond yesterday. I fear our short rations for man and horse will have to be curtailed. Our enemies have their troubles too. They are very strong immediately in front but have withdrawn their troops above and below us back toward Acquia Creek. I owe Mr. F.J. Hooker no thanks for keeping me here. He ought to have made up his mind long ago what to do–24th. The cars have arrived and brought me a young French officer full of vivacity and ardent for service with me. I think the appearance of things will cool him. If they do not the night will for he brought no blankets.

R.E. LEE

Excerpts from the diary of James J. Kirkpatrick, 16th Mississippi Infantry:

November 27th [1861]
Went on picket again at the same place. When the weather is fair, we now look forward to our picket tours, as ones of pleasure. No enemy near enough to circumscribe our foraging limits, and with more liberties than at camp, we rarely fail of having a good time. Camp life is becoming very monotonous at our present abode. Winter is near at hand, and our tents a very inadequate shelter for this cold clime. Wood too has become an object—far off and bad roads to haul it over. The cold winds, howling around us like evil spirits, admonish us to prepare for "worse coming." Chimneys of some structure, are built to our tents, but they afford us more smoke than heat. If to furnish smoke had been the object of their erection, no amount of skill could have succeeded better. We have not yet become proficient in camp architecture. Like true philosophers, we group around our smoky fires, jests and mirth pass around, duty is cheerfully performed, although our future prospects for comfort are gloomy indeed.

November 21st [1862]
Started at 8 A.M. After striking the plank road our march was easier. Passed Chancellorsville and camped within seven miles of Fredericksburg.

November 22nd [1862]
Marched briskly to Fredericksburg. Just as we came in view, the Yankees shelled back a train approaching from Richmond. The enemy's camps and wagons in plain view across the river. Many families from town passed us going to the rear. Filed to left of plank road and camped in line of battle.

Received orders to have our guns unloaded and dried out. On account of the many rains to which we had been exposed, few of them would fire. Regimental Inspection in the evening.

November 23rd [1862]
A pleasant morning but, somewhat cool. After breakfast took a stroll out to some of the hills to view the scenery and see what movements might be going on. Everything still and the only signs of the enemy are their tents and the smoke of their campfires in the Stafford Hills. A number of the boys went to town. The pickets at the river are on very good terms with each other, converse and pass jokes freely.

Letter from Lieutenant Thomas M. Hightower, Company D, 21ˢᵗ Georgia Volunteer Infantry, to a friend:

Jan 29, 1863
Camp near Fredericksburg

…Well, Lou, I have no camp news worth writing. We have had a big snow. It commenced snowing yesterday morning and continued until this morning covering the ground from one to three feet deep. Where it has not drifted it is three feet deep. There is a big snowballing going on now between our Regt. and the 12th. and 4th. Ga., they are both against ours. It is a pretty sight to see six or seven hundred men throwing snowballs. It is very good sport for me to look at them but I don't see much fun attached to handling the cold snow.

…We are in camps now about four miles from where we fought the battle on the 13th of December. We moved up here some four or five days ago and have had bad weather ever since we got here. We had very good quarters when we left and were living tolerable comfortably but where we moved to we found only a few pine pole cabins covered with dirt and we have the benefit of the weather since we have been here. It commenced raining the day after we moved and our house turned the water very well. The next day we went on picket and were gone for two days. When we came back we found it like pouring water through a griddle and it kept up until this morning when the snow ceased. We raked off the top of our cabin and it is not leaking so bad. It is right amusing to see how we have had to sleep the past two nights. Battle and I have a bunk in one corner and Wright and McCormick in the other. Our bed is composed of two forks driven in the ground and a pole put from one to the other. There are short poles from that to a crack in the wall with a small quantity of straw on

them and then our blankets and our humble selves upon that. That constitutes our house furniture. Then we lie down we spread our rubber cloths over us to keep the rain and snow off. We sleep as comfortably as if we were in one of the finest mansions in Cedar Valley. The floor of our cabin is six inches deep in mud and water except a little place around the fire. You will discern that a few drops of water have fallen on the paper.

Lieutenant Thomas M. Hightower

Letter from Samuel C. Clyde, 2nd South Carolina Infantry, to a friend:

Camp Near Fredericksburg, Va.
January 28, 1863

This is the first favorable moment I have had to reply to your last kind favor. On the same day that I received it we had to move camp some three miles, since which time we have been busily engaged in building temporary winter quarters. We have just completed our work and are now pretty comfortably situated and tolerably well prepared for stormy weather. Every one in the Company in fact the Regiment have been engaged in building some sort of quarters, and are now very snugly fixed, I cannot say how long we will be allowed to enjoy this comfort as the enemy have been making demonstrations at different points and threatening to attack us. We have twice recently received orders to cook up rations and have everything in readiness to move at a moments notice. The first order we paid but little attention to, as we could not believe the Yankees so foolish as to attempt another, offensive movement so soon after having received such a drumming as they got at Fredericksburg. But the second order was of such an alarming nature—as to cause us to believe they certainly meant something. They were in substance just the same as those issued a few days preceding the bloody fight that took place on the 13th December/62. The signal gun which was to summons us to prepare for action was heard early one morning a little before day dawn. We were aroused immediately by the "long roll" ordered to fall in. Before, however, we were formed, Gen'l Kershaw sent word to the Colonels to allow their men time to cook and eat something before marching. While breakfast was progressing a courier arrived with orders stating that it was a false alarm, and that the men could take off their trappings and make themselves comfortable. This was good news, of course, as the weather was cold and raining. We have had bad weather ever since and for this cause I presume they have postponed their attack upon our lines.

Judging from appearances no I think it will be sometime before they can make any offensive movement, as the ground is white with snow and it is still falling thick and fast and bids fair to continue some length of time. We are not sorry I assure you for to be exposed [to] such weather as this without fire would be almost death to us. If allowed to remain where we are, we can get along very well, as we all have very snug quarters with good chimneys to them. We are not indebted to the Government or any of its officials for these comforts, but they are the fruits of our own labors. We have not received but one tent from the Government as yet. Those we have we procured upon the battlefield from the Yankees. I am not disposed to complain, however, our Government has done a great deal. We get plenty to eat, such as it is, and the Army is at present well clothed, in better condition than it has ever been.

Ever Your Sincere Friend,
S.C.C.

Letter from John McDonald of the 13th Mississippi Infantry to his wife:

In camp near Fredericksburg
December the 9th, 1862
Mrs. Susan H. McDonald
My Dear Susan & children. Thank God I am still alive and able to write. It is no pleasure for me to write this evening for my eyes are nearly smoked out I never suffered as much with smoke in my life we have used up all the oak wood in reach of us now we are using green pine and it smokes our eyes almost out. Susan my health is much better than it was when I wrote last. [illegible] is enjoying the best health that he has since we left home he is off somewhere in the camps writeing. I and Martin both recieved a letter from you this morning you my depend on it that we were glad to here from you and to hear that you were all well. Joe Watters come in (this) yesterday and he brought me a letter and some money 10 dollars and my shirts and gloves. Susan I know you will be sory when I tell you that the gloves are too large in the hands and fingers. I hate the worse sort but however they will keep out cold thank you for them. Susan you sent the money I told you to keep for paying taxes although you through you was doing right the money ceom unwelcome to me. I had drawn 23 dollars foe my services I intend to send back the money that you sent me for I have 30 dollars without it the ballance of the boys drew their bounty and 2 months wages and I drew 2 months wages 23 dollars. I will send the 2 5's

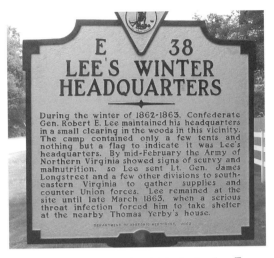

Roadside marker on Mine Road near Lee's Hill identifying the location of General Robert E. Lee's winter headquarters. *Courtesy of the Virginia Department of Historical Resources.*

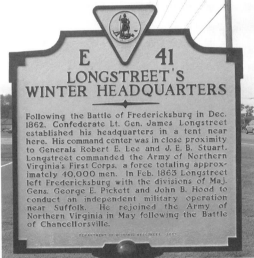

Roadside marker on Lafayette Boulevard near Spotswood Baptist Church Hill identifying the location of Lieutenant General James Longstreet's winter headquarters. *Courtesy of the Virginia Department of Historical Resources.*

Roadside marker on VA Route 1 identifying the location of cavalry commander General J.E.B. Stuart's winter camp. *Courtesy of the Virginia Department of Historical Resources.*

back that you sent me the verry 2 fives that I put away for you to pay taxes with the cotton 5 and Confederate 5. the cotton money is not current in this country no how dont understand me to be scolding you for your mistake my dear. If ever I get home I will kiss you for it I want to see you and the children verry much at this time Susan I sent you a lock of my hair while I was at Richmond I put it in after I had finished my letter and never said a word about it then and never could think to say anything about it. Susan I have read to the 11 chapter of St. John in the new testament let me know whether you got that lock of hair or not. Mr. Watters come in unexpected to all the boys Mary ann sent me a letter by Joe She wrote that she felt verry unwell at the time she wrote. I am afraid that she is sick. Susan my face is geting verry hairy I have not had a razor or scissors on my face since I left home my mustache is half as long as my finger. Susan I have no war news to write you at this time there is not a sick man in the company at this time that is a great thing for the army. Tell the old Lady Barnett that Joe is well and hearty, give my love and respects to my and your mothers family. I will close, may God bless you and my dears. I am your husband.
John McDonald

Reminiscences of Oliver J. Lehman, 33rd North Carolina Infantry:

About 4 months of the army was spent in Winter Quarters. The camp was laid out in streets running at right angles. The houses, or quarters as they were called, were of many styles of architecture—the most comfortable, were built out of logs, covered with split boards, which were held in place with heavy poles as no nails were to be had, & a stick chimney covered with mud. Others were about 4 feet high with logs covered with tent cloth. Officers usually occupied tents. If we were encamped on a hillside, quite a number lived in dugouts under ground. On fair days we did the usual camp duties as prescribed, such as drills & inspections, but by far the most of our time was occupied by writing letters, card playing, as only games, no gambling by other amusements. Every night that the weather was favorable, the Brigade, or 33rd Regt Band as it was called, was ordered to play one hour, & the cheers of the soldiers could be heard for miles around. Frequently after playing a few songs, a Yankee Band in our front could be heard playing some selection followed by yells from their comrades. The monotonous of camp life was often broken by one of our own men with a board strapped on their backs with the letters "I am a thief" or "I stole my comrade's rations" marching through the camp, up one street and down another with two drum corps in front of them making all possible noise to attract attention. Occasionally our boys were Court martialed for different offences & sentenced to walk in a circle about 50 feet in diameter, carrying on their shoulders a billet of wood weighing from 60 to 70 lbs for an hour each day, for a day or a week according to the offence. A guard with a musket stood by and kept him moving until his time expired.

This got to be a serious matter about the close of Winter. All the trees in and near camp were cut & used, next digging out the stumps and roots, & when they were all used, we had to carry wood for a mile or more on our shoulders. When camp was broken at the opening of the Spring and campaign or a battle was pending, the roads were strewn with playing cards, & hundreds of letters which our boys tore to pieces and threw away. A soldier did not like the idea of being killed with a pack of cards in his pocket, neither did he want anyone to read his letters.

In late 1862 and through early 1863, Spotsylvania County hosted several significant winter quarters as the Army of Northern Virginia had been operating in the area throughout the end of the year. After defeating Federal forces on December 12 and 13 in the Battle of Fredericksburg, the Confederate army set up camps in the surrounding area. These included the winter quarters of General Robert E. Lee, General James Longstreet and cavalry commander General J.E.B. Stuart. Today, three Virginia Roadside Markers stand along Route 1 in the Lee's Hill area marking these locations. They read as follows:

Lee's Winter Headquarters E-38: During the winter of 1862–1863, Confederate Gen. Robert E. Lee maintained his headquarters in a small clearing in the woods in this vicinity. The camp contained only a few tents and nothing but a flag to indicate it was Lee's headquarters. By mid-February the Army of Northern Virginia showed signs of scurvy and malnutrition, so Lee sent Lt. Gen. James Longstreet and a few other divisions to southeastern Virginia to gather supplies and counter Union forces. Lee remained at the site until late March 1863, when a serious throat infection forced him to take shelter at the nearby Thomas Yerby's house.

Longstreet's Winter Headquarters E-41: Following the Battle of Fredericksburg in Dec. 1862, Confederate Lt. Gen. James Longstreet established his headquarters in a tent near here. His command center was in close proximity to Generals Robert E. Lee and J.E.B. Stuart. Longstreet commanded the Army of Northern Virginia's First Corps, a force totaling approximately 40,000

Confederate General James Longstreet, commander of the 1st Corps, Army of Northern Virginia. *Courtesy of the Library of Congress.*

men. In Feb. 1863 Longstreet left Fredericksburg with the divisions of Maj. Gens. George E. Pickett and John B. Hood to conduct an independent military operation near Suffolk. He rejoined the Army of Northern Virginia in May following the Battle of Chancellorsville.

Stuart E-8: At this point J.E.B. Stuart had his headquarters and cavalry camp in December 1862.

It is understandable that troops who were stuck in winter quarters would search for new forms of merriment in order to break up their day-to-day routines. Although a thick blanket of snow made for uncomfortable sleeping arrangements, it did allow men to be boys. Sometimes snowball fights would erupt, pitting large groups of soldiers against one another. It has been said that the largest military snow exchange occurred in Northern Virginia on January 29, 1863, when a group of Texans initiated a battle against their compatriots from Arkansas. The melee spilled over into other camps and resulted in a scuffle involving over nine thousand soldiers from the Army of Northern Virginia. Similar friendly engagements took place across the county of Spotsylvania.

Entry from the journal of John Elsten Cooke, staff officer with General J.E.B. Stuart, Army of Northern Virginia Cavalry:

Camp "No Camp" (Spotsylvania, VA)

Jan 30th '63…A great snowball battle among the Brigades which was worth seeing. Yesterday Hood's Texans & Georgians issued from their camp near Lee's Hdqrs. and led by Gen. [Brigadier General Micah] *Jenkins attacked and routed* [Brigadier General Joseph B.] *Kershaw's S.C. Carolinians camped toward Mrs. Alsop's. Inflamed with victory the Hood boys today advanced in battle array with flags flying and led by their officers against* [Brigadier General Thomas R.R.] *Cobb of* [Major General Lafayette] *McLaw's Div. (as Kershaw is). The camp is just back of ours in the pines. The scene was a lively and funny one. The Hoodites charged into the camp, drove out the Andersonites* [Wofford] *and put them to rout. But they rallied got reinforcements, and drove the Hoodites from the woods, across the Telegraph road, and into the fields, with storms of balls (snow).*

What was the horror of the Hoodites to see Kershaw's men, drawn up on their left flank, ready to attack. They halted and their leader rode forward and parlayed—he demanded assistance against a common foe—the Yankee Anderson [Wofford]*. A long parlay, refused at first, but compliance at last, and the combined forces attacked the enemy. Anderson was drawn up on the crest of a hill, and fought with desperation but numbers overpowered him. He fell back in confusion, his foes pursued; and burst into his camp. "Come on boys!" was the cry "here's your blankets, your cooking utensils, and everything!" Some thought they were in earnest. Then Hood as usual conquered.*

The scene was a very good mimic battle. The men advanced and fell back, deployed, and charged—turned the enemy's flank, and "carried on" generally like real fighters. They had guidons for flags; and the regiments marched in very good order to the battle. There were many officers galloping about with irresistible air of leading their men—others were shouting in furious tones to stragglers—and snow balls flew as thick as leaves in an autumn wind. I saw it from horseback and laughed heartily I think I will write it out for the Whig or the News.

Rebel Recollections

News and Views from the Front Lines

Oftimes however, we would be ragged in clothes and almost shoeless.
It is a fact that our army generally was almost barefooted on our
Maryland Campaign.
—*Captain Wilson T. Jenkins, 14ᵗʰ North Carolina Infantry*

Throughout the course of military history, soldiers in every army and every conflict wrote letters and kept diaries while on campaign. For many, this was the only way to maintain a connection to the life that they longed to return to at home. It was also a form of escapism, a way to forget about the hardships that surrounded them and helped them to maintain an act of normalcy amidst the abnormal existence of war. "Mail call" has always been one of the most anticipated events in army camps from the days of Napoleon to today. Troops in the Confederate army were no different, and in an attempt to share their experiences with friends and family, they unwittingly recorded their own legacy. From battle reports and testaments to camp gossip and death notifications, the average soldier in the Army of Northern Virginia played the role of newsman, similar to today's embedded journalist.

Recollections from Captain Wilson T. Jenkins of the 14ᵗʰ North Carolina Infantry:

Battle of Fredericksburg.
Camp near Rappahannock.

With our several duties there was no great amount of idle time to the private soldiers. When not employed, we played cards, walked, talked, pitched quoits, wrote letters, and read. Whenever settled in camp, Richmond papers were received daily, as a result of which Virginia Editors gave tone to many of the impressions of commands, officers and events. We also visited our friends in other camps, went swimming in Chickahominy, Bull Run, etc. Under Act of Confederate Congress, soldiers could send their letters without prepaying postage, which was paid on receipt, by writing his name and command on the upper left hand corner.

…We improvised coverings of blankets, shawls, waterproofs etc. In cold weather we generally built our fires in front of our tents. We kept warm by standing near the fire, constantly changing our position with the wind to get out of the smoke—some times not soon enough to keep our clothes from getting scorched. Once near Fredericksburg, having been up all night before on guard duty, I went to sleep covered with a blanket, my covered feet projecting beyond the tent opening. When I awoke I was covered up to my knees with snow. At this place, Gen. Longstreet sent down an order one day to remove their fires at night and spread their blankets on the warm ground. This order was not universally obeyed; the few who did it the first night proved the impracticability of the order.

We were supposed to be clothed, shod and blanketed by the Confederate government, but the quartermaster's stores were not abundant. We kept up pretty well in underclothing and the charitable and patriotic women at home would sometimes send a box to a company, and individuals were not forgot by the loved ones at home. Oftimes however, we would be ragged in clothes and almost shoeless. It is a fact that our army generally was almost barefooted on our Maryland Campaign. We were first paid off in the Fall of 1861, for four months as I remember, the currency then being the bills of State banks. After that our pay day was about every two months when we received Confederate money, which had begun to depreciate as early as 1862 and was worse by the beginning of 1863.

Gambling was common though I was free from this vice. In the winter of 1861, chuck-a-luck was rampant. We had company chuck-a-luck, regimental chuck-a-luck, brigade chuck-a-luck and division chuck-a-luck. The tent of the last named was nicely carpeted. Raffling was also a mania, and men raffled everything they could spare—rings, pistols, watches etc. The fairest raffle I

Illustration of soldiers chasing a rabbit that wandered into their camp. *Courtesy of the Fredericksburg/Spotsylvania NMPS.*

knew was a $20 bill—25 chances at $1 a chance. There was also too much drinking particularly among the officers.

And I ought not to omit mention of the pestiferous body lice. Some men were so dirty and some places so foul, that no one could keep entirely away from them. I managed to be almost free of them in my tent, but when sent out on picket where others had been before, I would be sure to come back with a good supply in the seams of my clothing.

On returning to camp, I would strip off and clean off, but I would be again infected on the next trip away.

It was now cold and rainy with some falls of snow. We had our usual camp duties, going out sometimes on picket. We could see the enemy across the river. On November 28th, the 15th S.C. regiment (Col. W.D. DeSaussure) and James Battalion were added to Kershaw's Brigade. On 3rd and 4th December we were looking for a battle, and under orders to march at the firing of signal guns, but the two days passed without the signals. On the 5th it rained and snowed, and that night we had an eclipse of the moon. On same day I received the box that had been shipped to me from home in August, and also an overcoat from Tami Tounce (?) at a recent date. The box had been opened and some of its contents stolen but the thief must have been a teetotaler as he left untouched a bottle of brandy.

Recollections of Sergeant J.J. McDaniel, Company M, 7th South Carolina Infantry:

[Prior to the Battle of Fredericksburg]
We staid near Culpeper a few days and I fully recovered my health. From there we marched to Fredericksburg. Here we took up camp on the hills overlooking the city on the Telegraph Road. We did picket duty in the city; were cooped up in warehouses. One evening we were ordered on picket below the city on the Rappahannock River. The snow was falling rapidly, we were poorly clothed and shod. We were put on duty without fire on the post but could have a little fire at the reserve post but had no wood. I stole a lot of corn and fodder that night to make me a bed on which to sleep when the on post and a plow stocks to make a fire. It cleared up about 12 o'clock, cold enough for any purpose. The night finally passed away and we were relieved and returned to camp. Burnside finally commenced to throw pontoon bridges across the river, and was met by Barksdale Mississippi Brigade. Hundreds of shell was poured into the town and finally Barksdale was recalled and preparations were made for the final struggle. The signal cannon was fired and Lee's veteran army moved to its place along the line.

[Following the Battle of Chancellorsville]
Fighting Joe Hooker had enough and that night crossed the river. We went back to our camp near Fredericksburg. We were always scarce of lead and I was sent as one of a detail to pick up lead on the field. About half way between where the fighting first started, at Salem church, I found two—minnie balls. One had been fired by the Federals and one by the Confederates. They had struck each other so true that they had become imbedded into each other, and fell to the ground. While our troops were at Fredericksburg during the winter, one night a Federal band got to playing; then the Yankees would cheer their bands. Then one of our bands would play a piece and our boys would. Finally both bands continued to play Home Sweet Home and if it had not been for the officers the war would have stopped that night and all the soldiers would have gone home.

Diary entry of Noah Collins of the 37th North Carolina Infantry:

After remaining at the White House Hospital, in Danville Pittsylvania County Virginia, thirty nine days, suffering a great many changes of disease, such as all sorts of Diarrhea, neuralgia and dropsy, I left that place by rail, on the

12th day of December 1862, and went to my command, near Fredericksburg, Spotsylvania County Virginia; at which place I arrived, late in the evening of the 13th instant, and found none but the sick, and a few of the wounded in camps; in consequence of all the bale soldiers being engaged on that day, in the flagitious or grossly wicked Battle of Fredericksburg...On the morning of the 14th instant I left the camps of the 37th North Carolina Regiment, and started down to the Battlefield of Fredericksburg, Spotsylvania County Virginia, to rejoin my command, but did not more than fairly get in range of the skirmish balls of the winding up of the fight, till I met the old 37th North Carolina Regiment, coming out of the battlefield, when I turned my course and went back with the Regiment to the oldcamps, it occupied before the fight; very much gratified to find so many of the company unharmed; at which place we did not remain more than one hour, till we continued our march about four miles down the Rappahannock River, in Spotsylvania County Virginia, and encamped on the same day. During our sojourn or stay at that place we suffered inexpressibly or indescribably in consequence of our being exposed as we were, to the intensely cold weather and smoke of the camp fires that prevailed or took place at that place.

After remaining at this place of torment, thirty two days, we left it on foot, on the 15th day of January 1863, and went about one mile North West of that place, up the Rappahannock River, to Camp Gregg, of the same County and State; at which place we arrived on the same day; and bettered our fare a little by constructing ourselves huts to stay in and shelter us from the weather. During our sojourn of stay at this place we suffered to an alarming extent, in the performance of so much unnecessary camp guard duty; in the intense cold weather, rain and snow, that prevailed or followed so profusely or abundantly at that place. After remaining at Camp Gregg, near Fredericksburg, Spotsylvania County Virginia, three months and fourteen days; we left that place on foot, on the 29th day of April 1863, and went to the old Battlefield of Fredericksburg, Spotsylvania County Virginia, and fortified ourselves, under the shells of Union Artillery. Next day which was the 30th instant, we left that place and went down the plank road till we met the Union troops under general Joseph Hooker, but we did not become engaged at that place.

(The author then went on to be wounded and captured during the Battle of Chancellorsville, before being rescued by fellow Confederates and taken to a field hospital. He later returned to Spotsylvania County to fight in the Battle of the Wilderness in 1864.)

Southern soldiers and servant posing in front of one of their tents. *Courtesy of the Library of Congress.*

Letter from Second Lieutenant John D. Dameron, Company K, 49th North Carolina Infantry (later 4th Regiment Cavalry), to his father:

Fredericksburg, Va.
Dec. 17th, 1862
Dear Father,
I had concluded that I could not write to you any more until I had received a letter from home. But, I came to the conclusion that this course of procedure bid fair to cut off all communication whatever. As I have given up all idea of receiving a scaratch from your very reserved pen. You certainly should be appointed Superintendent over some asylum of mutes, as I verily believe your experience in such matters would be highly beneficial to such an institution.

Above: Sketch of the Spotsylvania Court House area. *Lee Foundation.*

Below: Troops camped near the Spotsylvania Court House. *Courtesy of the Fredericksburg/ Spotsylvania NMPS.*

We have had another great Battle at this place resulting in a decisive victory for the Confederate Army. Fredericksburg was shelled on Thursday 11th Dec. On Friday there was little done, except a continual fire of artillery. On Saturday the battle oppined [sic] *early in the morning on the right of our lines. Where Old Stone-fence commanded, 15 min. before 11 A.M. the Battle commenced near and around the city. The small arms made one continual roar without a moment's cessation from 15 before 11 until dark. Our position was splendid.*

It is said we were attacked by 40,000 Federals at this point. Whilst our force which opposed them did not amount to one 4th of that number. there were about 30 acres covered with [illegible line due to fold in letter] *very small. tis said that we repulsed them 17 different times, each charge being made with overwhelming numbers. Their loss is estimated at 20,000 in killed & wounded, whilst ours will not exceed 2500. 500 of which was killed. Most of our killed was on the right where Stone-fence fought them. The slaughter on the right is said to exceed anything of the war. If it was greater than around the city, it must have been awful. Near the city we lost Generals Cobb of GA & Maxwell Gregg of ALA. The Federals loss in killed may be fairly estimated at 6000. 14,000 wounded & about 3000 prisoners. I understand Burnside has reopened the river to its northern bank, removing their pontoon bridges 5 in number & withdrawing their troops from view. Only a few remaining in sight. What will be Burnsides next move is not known. But, supposed that he will try Port Royal on the Rappahonock some 50 miles from this place down the river. There are various conjectures. He will be closely watched by Gen. Lee, who has the entire confidence of the Southern Army. Our army is in fine condition & went into the fight on Saturday with perfect cheerfulness. This was the best (strgling???) ever known. every man stood to his post & fought bravely. I narrowly escaped being killed by the explosion of a shell.*

I have not anything more that would interest you. Col McAffee is well, & etc. Ellison. Black was wounded in the head by a ball or piece of shell & is now on his way to Richmond. His wound is not serious. He may be home before long. I have not received the clothing mother sent me. The boxes were sent here from Richmond the day we were ordered to the battlefield & we could not get them. Some were sent back & some are scattered every where. We will probably never see them. Tell sister Ann I got that letter she wrote me last week, but my eyes were so bad that I could not make out anything that was not in it. Tell Sallie to write. She owes me one. All of you write, or you may consider this my last. I never expect to get home again at all. Furloughs are out of

date. They would sell for 500. Money is worth nothing & nothing is worth
everything. My love to all & little Gill especially.
Your son, affectionately,
Jno D. Dameron

Letter from Adam W. Kersh, 20th Virginia Cavalry, to his brother:

George P Kersh
Fredericksburg, VA
May 24, 1863

Dear Brother
I received your letter on the 22nd and was glad to hear from you all at home.
We have a good many troops camped about us here. It is thought that the
Yankees intend to try us again here
Since they found out that Jackson is dead. It is said that they appear keen
to try us again. It is true we have lost a good General, but we still have a few
more smart men left let them come. I don't believe that they are as anxious
to fight as they let on to be. Just mere talk they have the advantage of us at
Fredericksburg on account of the big number of siege guns they have planted
there. As long as they are under shelter of them they can talk large. Just let
them advance and we are ready for them, we got a great many guns knapsacks
shovels picks and such things in the last fight. They been sending them off
from the depot Hamilton's Crossing ever since the fight. It is a detail made
in our regiment of about twenty five men every day to help unload and load
the cars. It is also details made out of other regiments in our Brigade to stand
guard and fatigue duty. It is a good many old suttlers at the Station. They sell
very high too beans, one dollar a quart, one dollar for about a quart of irish
potatoes, and other things in proportion. It is awful warm here now, has been
for several days, we have no shade the timber has all been cut for firewood.
We expect to move out of our cabins in a few days about a half mile in the
woods in the shade.
We have tolerable good water here, but not as Good and cool as in Augusta.
Our Mess got ourselves good little tents and knapsacks and blankets in the last
fight it was thousands of old United States blankets and little tents scattered
over the battle field. I sent a letter by John Hale to male in Staunton or Sidney,
which I suppose you have received by this time.
You were speaking of coming down. I did not look for you as you have
nobody capable of attending to your business and a busy time too. You were

Confederate soldier who fell in Spotsylvania. *Courtesy of the Library of Congress.*

speaking of Cavalry taking quarters in my house. I have no objections so long as they act like gentlemen. You were speaking of the people being panic struck and come flocking through Mount Crawford by the thousand. I do hope that we, our men, will be able to put the thing through soon and that folks might go home and have some peace. Fredericksburg is pretty much torn to pieces with shells the most of the citizens have moved away a great many houses has been entirely destroyed.

Me and some of the boys took a walk over the battlefield at Fredericksburg before the last fight, we could see plenty of old half decayed Yankees some with their heads sticking out arms hands and feet sticking out it was awful sight to behold.

As I have nothing much to write about. I will close I am well and hope these few lines may find you all in good health…

Your affectionate brother
Adam W Kersh

Perhaps no other transcript in this collection better represents the sacrifice of soldiers who were encamped in the Spotsylvania area than this letter penned by Private James Robert Montgomery. Private Montgomery was a courier enlisted in Company A of the 11th Mississippi Infantry. On May 10, 1864, he was struck by a shell fragment while attempting to deliver communications for General Heth. As he lay dying from a mortal wound, he wrote the following letter to his father:

Spotsylvania County, Va.
May 10

Dear Father
This is my last letter to you. I went into battle this evening as courier for Genl. Heth. I have been struck by a piece of shell and my right shoulder is horribly mangled & I know death is inevitable. I am very weak but I write to you because I know you would be delighted to read a word from your dying son. I know death is near, that I will die far from home and friends of my early youth but I have friends here too who are kind to me. My friend Fairfax will write you at my request and give you the particulars of my death. My grave will be marked so that you may visit it if you desire to do so, but it is optionary with you whether you let my remains rest here or in Miss. I would like to rest in the grave yard with my dear mother and brothers but it's a matter of minor importance. Let us all try to reunite in heaven. I pray my God to forgive my sins and I feel that his promises are true that he will forgive me and save me. Give my love to all my friends. My strength fails me. My horse and my equipments will be left for you. Again, a long farewell to you. May we meet in heaven.

Your dying son,
J.R. Montgomery

SUMMATION

The Bivouac in the Snow

Referred to today as the "Poet of the Confederacy," Margaret Junkin Preston penned several memorable verses recounting life in the pre- and postwar South. As the sister of Elinore Junkin Jackson, the first wife of General Thomas Jonathan "Stonewall" Jackson, she also married a professor (J.L.T. Preston), from the Virginia Military Institute in Lexington, Virginia. Following the South's surrender, Margaret became a published writer and was eventually anthologized in several early twentieth-century collections of Southern poetry. This poem, albeit venerating in tone, captured the experiences of Confederate soldiers in camp:

The Bivouac in the Snow
by Margaret Junkin Preston

Halt!—the march is over,
  Day is almost done;
Loose the cumbrous knapsack,
  Drop the heavy gun.
Chilled and wet and weary,
  Wander to and fro,
Seeking wood to kindle
  Fires amidst the snow.

Illustration depicting a Confederate sentry on guard at winter camp. *Courtesy of the Valentine Museum, Richmond.*

The Bivouac in the Snow

Round the bright blaze gather,
  Heed not sleet or cold;
Ye are Spartan soldiers,
  Stout and brave and bold.
Never Xerxian army
  Yet subdued a foe
Who but asked a blanket
  On a bed of snow.

Shivering, 'midst the darkness,
  Christian men are found,
There devoutly kneeling
  On the frozen ground—
Pleading for their country,
  In its hour of woe—
For the soldiers marching
  Shoeless through the snow.

Lost in heavy slumbers,
  Free from toil and strife,
Dreaming of their dear ones—
  Home, and child, and wife—
Tentless they are lying,
  While the fires burn low—
Lying in their blankets
  'Midst December's snow.

Appendix

ARMY OF NORTHERN VIRGINIA

CAMP REGISTER

Listing of Confederate Units

T he challenge of pinpointing the exact geographical locations of all Confederate encampments in Spotsylvania County and the surrounding regions remains a difficult one. According to sources at the National Park Service, occupying armies did not take time to map something as mundane as campsites. Most mapmakers were focused on developing functional maps rather than retrospective ones. Military cartographers and topographers such as Jedediah Hotchkiss were tasked with mapping out campaign sites and some battlefields. The NPS added that the Federal forces were much better at identifying their camp locations, most of which are known today, while the Confederate troops have little or no official records on the subject. A few Southern camps have been noted, such as Camp Mercer, a recruiting and training ground that was located on the site of Fredericksburg's former fairgrounds, as well as Camp Gregg, which was located about eight miles south of the city in Spotsylvania County. Some units inhabited the ruins of the city of Fredericksburg. Other locations include campsites located near major landmarks such as Salem Church. Many soldiers simply listed their locations on letters to loved ones as "Camp in Fredericksburg" and "Near Spotsylvania Court House."

Despite this difficulty, we are able to identify which troops from the Army of Northern Virginia were amassed during engagements in the Fredericksburg/ Spotsylvania area from 1861 through 1864 and can assume with relative

Above: Confederate officer portrait. *Courtesy of the Library of Congress.*

Opposite, top: Company A of the 5th Georgia Volunteers and their servant lounge in front of a wall tent. *Courtesy of the Library of Congress.*

Opposite, bottom: Members of the Washington Artillery, Louisiana's oldest militia unit, muster in camp. *Courtesy of the Van Pelt Library.*

confidence that they were encamped there. By using the Orders of Battle from each of the four engagements, we can identify what forces from the ANV were present. This does not account for every Southern unit that may have passed through the county during the course of the Civil War, but it does give a good impression of the majority of units that were represented in local camps.

The following units were present during the Battle of Fredericksburg in December 1862; the Battle of Chancellorsville in April and May 1863; and the Battles of the Wilderness and Spotsylvania Court House in May 1864.

All were encamped at one time or another in Spotsylvania County and the surrounding region.

ALABAMA

3rd Alabama Infantry
4th Alabama Infantry
5th Alabama Battalion
5th Alabama Infantry
6th Alabama Infantry
8th Alabama Infantry
9th Alabama Infantry
10th Alabama Infantry
11th Alabama Infantry
12th Alabama Infantry
13th Alabama Infantry
14th Alabama Infantry
15th Alabama Infantry
26th Alabama Infantry
44th Alabama Infantry
47th Alabama Infantry
48th Alabama Infantry
Hardaway's Battery
Hurt's Battery
Reese's, Jeff Davis Battery

ARKANSAS

3rd Arkansas Infantry

FLORIDA

2nd Florida Infantry
5th Florida Infantry
8th Florida Infantry

GEORGIA

1st Georgia (Regulars)
2nd Georgia Battalion
2nd Georgia Infantry
3rd Battalion Sharpshooters
3rd Georgia Infantry
4th Georgia Infantry
6th Georgia Infantry
7th Georgia Infantry
8th Georgia Infantry
9th Georgia Cavalry (Cobb's Legion)
9th Georgia Infantry
10th Georgia Infantry
11th Georgia Infantry
12th Georgia Infantry
13th Barlow Light Infantry
13th Georgia Infantry
14th Georgia Infantry
15th Georgia Infantry
16th Georgia Infantry
16th Sallie Twiggs Regiment
17th Georgia Infantry
18th Georgia Infantry
18th Georgia (Savannah Volunteer Guards)
19th Georgia Infantry
20th Georgia Battalion
20th Georgia Infantry
21st Georgia Infantry
22nd Georgia Infantry
23rd Georgia Infantry
24th Georgia Infantry
26th Georgia Infantry
27th Georgia Infantry
28th Georgia Infantry
31st Georgia Infantry
35th Georgia Infantry
38th Georgia Infantry
44th Georgia Infantry
45th Georgia Infantry

48th Georgia Infantry
49th Georgia Infantry
50th Georgia Infantry
51st Georgia Infantry
53rd Georgia Infantry
59th Georgia Infantry
60th Georgia Infantry
61st Georgia Infantry
Callaway's Battery
Carlton's Troup Artillery Battery
Ells's Battery
Fraser's Pulaski Battery
Milledge's Battery
Patterson's Sumter, Battery B
Phillips's Georgia Legion (Cavalry)
Read's Battery
Ross's Sumter, Battery A
Troup's Artillery
Wingfield's Battery

LOUISIANA

1st Louisiana Infantry
1st Louisiana Infantry (Volunteers)
2nd Louisiana Infantry
2nd Louisiana Infantry (Zouaves)
5th Louisiana Infantry
6th Louisiana Infantry
7th Louisiana Infantry (Pelican Regiment)
8th Louisiana Infantry
9th Louisiana Infantry
10th Louisiana Infantry
14th Louisiana (1st Regiment Polish Brigade)
15th Louisiana (2nd Regiment Polish Brigade)
Coppens's Battalion
Donaldsonville Artillery
Eshleman's Fourth Company
Landry's Battery

Louisiana Guard Artillery
Madison Light Artillery
Miller's Third Company
Moody's Madison Battery
Richardson's Second Company
Squires First Company
Washington Artillery Battalion

MARYLAND

1st Maryland Cavalry
Brown's 4th Maryland Chesapeake Battery
Carrington's Chesapeake Artillery
Dement's First Maryland Battery
First Maryland Battery

MISSISSIPPI

2nd Mississippi Infantry
11th Mississippi Infantry
12th Mississippi Infantry
13th Mississippi Infantry
16th Mississippi Infantry
17th Mississippi Infantry
18th Mississippi Infantry
19th Mississippi Infantry
21st Mississippi Infantry
42nd Mississippi Infantry
48th Mississippi Infantry
Richards's Battery

NORTH CAROLINA

1st Battalion North Carolina Sharpshooters
1st North Carolina Battalion
1st North Carolina Cavalry

1st North Carolina Cavalry (9th Volunteers)
1st North Carolina Infantry
1st North Carolina (State Troops)
2nd North Carolina Battalion
2nd North Carolina Cavalry
2nd North Carolina Infantry
2nd North Carolina (State Troops)
3rd North Carolina Infantry
3rd North Carolina (State Troops)
4th North Carolina Infantry
4th North Carolina (State Troops)
5th North Carolina Infantry
5th North Carolina (State Troops)
6th North Carolina Infantry
6th North Carolina (State Troops)
7th North Carolina Infantry
7th North Carolina (State Troops)
11th North Carolina Infantry
12th North Carolina Infantry
13th North Carolina Infantry
14th North Carolina Infantry
15th North Carolina Infantry
16th North Carolina Infantry
18th North Carolina Infantry
20th North Carolina Infantry
21st North Carolina Infantry
22nd North Carolina Infantry
23rd North Carolina Infantry
24th North Carolina Infantry
25th North Carolina Infantry
26th North Carolina Infantry
27th North Carolina Infantry
28th North Carolina Infantry
30th North Carolina Infantry
32nd North Carolina Infantry
33rd North Carolina Infantry
34th North Carolina Infantry
35th North Carolina Infantry
37th North Carolina Infantry

38th North Carolina Infantry
43rd North Carolina Infantry
44th North Carolina Infantry
45th North Carolina Infantry
46th North Carolina Infantry
47th North Carolina Infantry
48th North Carolina Infantry
49th North Carolina Infantry
52nd North Carolina Infantry
53rd North Carolina Infantry
54th North Carolina Infantry
55th North Carolina Infantry
57th North Carolina Infantry
Flanner's Battery
Manly's North Carolina Battery
Ramsay's Battery
Rowan Artillery
Williams's Battery

South Carolina

1st South Carolina Cavalry
1st South Carolina Infantry
2nd Palmetto Sharpshooters
2nd South Carolina Cavalry
2nd South Carolina Infantry
2nd South Carolina (Rifles)
3rd South Carolina Battalion
3rd South Carolina Infantry
4th South Carolina Cavalry
5th South Carolina Cavalry
5th South Carolina Infantry
6th South Carolina Cavalry
6th South Carolina Infantry
7th South Carolina Infantry
8th South Carolina Infantry
12th South Carolina Infantry
13th South Carolina Infantry

14th South Carolina Infantry
15th South Carolina Infantry
Brunson's Pee Dee Battery
Fickling's Battery
Garden's Battery
German Artillery
Hart's Battery
Palmetto Light Artillery
Rhett's Brooks Battery
Washington Battery
Zimmerman's Battery

TENNESSEE

1st Tennessee Infantry (Provisional Army)
7th Tennessee Infantry
14th Tennessee Infantry

TEXAS

1st Texas Infantry
4th Texas Infantry
5th Texas Infantry

VIRGINIA

1st Stuart Horse Artillery
1st Virginia Battalion
1st Virginia Cavalry
1st Virginia Infantry
2nd Stuart Horse Artillery
2nd Virginia Cavalry
2nd Virginia Infantry
3rd Virginia Cavalry
3rd Virginia Infantry
4th Virginia Cavalry

4th Virginia Infantry
5th Virginia Cavalry
5th Virginia Infantry
6th Virginia Cavalry
6th Virginia Infantry
7th Virginia Cavalry
7th Virginia Infantry
8th Virginia Infantry
9th Virginia Cavalry
9th Virginia Infantry
10th Virginia Cavalry
10th Virginia Infantry
11th Virginia Cavalry
11th Virginia Infantry
12th Virginia Cavalry
12th Virginia Infantry
13th Virginia Cavalry
13th Virginia Infantry
14th Virginia Infantry
15th Virginia Cavalry
15th Virginia Infantry
16th Virginia Infantry
17th Virginia Battalion Cavalry
17th Virginia Infantry
18th Virginia Infantry
19th Virginia Infantry
21st Virginia Infantry
22nd Virginia Battalion
23rd Virginia Infantry
24th Virginia Infantry
25th Virginia Infantry
27th Virginia Infantry
28th Virginia Infantry
30th Virginia Infantry
31st Virginia Infantry
32nd Virginia Infantry
33rd Virginia Infantry
34th Virginia Battalion Cavalry
35th Virginia Battalion Cavalry

35th Virginia Battalion Infantry
37th Virginia Infantry
38th Virginia Infantry
40th Virginia Infantry
41st Virginia Infantry
42nd Virginia Infantry
44th Virginia Infantry
47th Virginia Infantry
48th Virginia Infantry
49th Virginia Infantry
50th Virginia Infantry
52nd Virginia Infantry
53rd Virginia Infantry
55th Virginia Infantry
56th Virginia Infantry
57th Virginia Infantry
58th Virginia Infantry
61st Virginia Infantry
Amherst Battery
Bedford Artillery
Branch's Battery
Brander's Battery
Breathed's Battery
Brooke's Warrenton Battery
Carpenter's Alleghany Battery
Carrington's Charlottesville Battery
Carter's King William Battery
Carter's W.P. Battery
Cayce's Battery
Charlottesville Artillery
Chew's Battery
Clutter's Battery
Cooper's Battery
Courtney Artillery
Crenshaw Battery
Dance's Battery (Powhatan Artillery)
Danville Artillery
Davidson's Letcher Battery
Dearing's Battery

Donald's Battery
Ellett's Battery
Eubank's Bath Battery
Fauquier Artillery
Fluvanna Artillery
Fredericksburg Artillery
Fry's Orange Battery
Garber's Stauton Battery
Graham's 1st Rockbridge Battery
Grandy's Norfolk Blues Battery
Hampden Artillery
Hanover Artillery
Hardwicke's Battery
Henry's Battery
Huger's Battery
Hupp's Salem Battery
Johnson's Richmond Battery
Jones's Battery
Jordan's Bedford Battery
King William Artillery
Kirkpatrick's Amherst Battery
Lamkin's Battery
Latimer's Courtney Battery
Lee Artillery
Letcher Artillery
Lewis's Pittsylvania Battery
Lusk's 2nd Rockbridge Battery
Lynchburg Beauregard's Battery
Marye's Battery
Massie's Fluvanna Battery
Maurin's Donaldsonville Battery
McCarthy's Battery
McGraw's Purcell Battery
McGregor's Battery
Moore's Norfolk Battery
Moorman's Battery
Morris Artillery
Norfolk Light Artillery Blues
Orange Artillery

Page's Morris Louisa Battery
Parker's Richmond Battery
Penick's Battery
Price's Battery
Purcell Artillery
Raine's Lee Battery
Richmond Fayette Artillery
Rockbridge Artillery
Salem Artillery
Shoemaker's Battery
Smith's, B.H. Battery
Smith's, J.D. Battery
Smith's Richmond Howitzer's 3rd Company
Staunton Artillery
Tanner's Battery
Taylor's Battery
Thomson's Battery
Utterback's Battery
Watson's Richmond Howitzers, 2nd Company
Wooding's Danville Battery
Woolfolk's Ashland Battery
Wyatt's Battery

Bibliography

Chancellor, Sue. *Personal Recollections of the Battle of Chancellorsville.* Compiled by Mrs. Emily W. Fleming. Fredericksburg, VA, n.d.

Civil War Society. *The Civil War Society's Encyclopedia of the Civil War—The Complete and Comprehensive Guide to the American Civil War.* N.p.: Portland House, 1997.

Cooke, John Esten. *Stonewall Jackson: A Military Biography.* Ann Arbor: Scholarly Publishing Office, University of Michigan Library, December 2005.

Hamilton, Matilda. *Diary of Matilda Hamilton (1817–1875) of Forest Hill.* Hamilton Family Papers, 1857–1880. Mss1H1805a. Virginia Historical Society.

Jones, J. William. *Christ in the Camp—Religion in Lee's Army.* N.p.: Diggory Press, 2006.

Lee, Robert E. *Recollections and Letters of General Robert E. Lee.* N.p.: Konecky & Konecky, 1998.

Manarin, Louis H., Weymouth T. Jordon Jr. *North Carolina Troops, 1861–1865, A Roster, Vol. V. Infantry, 11th–15th Regiments, 13th Battalion.* Raleigh, NC: State Division of Archives and History, 1990.

McCarthy, Carlton. *Detailed Minutiae of Soldier Life in the Army of Northern Virginia, Private of Second Company Richmond Howitzers, Cutshaw's Battalion.* Parts 1–3. Lincoln: University of Nebraska Press, 1993. Reprint, n.p.: Kessinger Publishing Company, 2008.

Robertson, James I., Jr. *Tenting Tonight.* New York: Time-Life Books, 1984.

Scott, Bradford Ripley Alden. *Memoirs of the Civil War.* Fredericksburg/ Spotsylvania National Military Park Service transcripts.

Southern Historical Society Papers 2, no. 3 (September 1876). Richmond, VA.

———— 2, no. 5 (September 1876). Richmond, VA.

———— 3, no. 1 (January 1877). Richmond, VA.

University of Notre Dame, Department of Special Collections. Letters of William W. Sillers (1863).

VMI Archives Manuscript #221: Samuel S. Brooke Papers.

Welch, Spencer Glasgow. *A Confederate Surgeon's Letters to His Wife.* N.p.: Neale Publishing Company, 1911.

MANUSCRIPTS

Excerpts from bound volumes from the Fredericksburg/Spotsylvania Military Park Service:

BV# 002-07: *Reminiscences of Roanoke Minute Men*, Company A, 14th North Carolina Troops.

BV# 002-09: Reminiscences of Oliver J. Lehman, 33rd North Carolina.

BV# 027-02: Misc. Letters from Simeon David, 14th North Carolina.

BV# 027-09: Hampton Legion, Head Qrs of the Legion. Camp Bartow, March 17, 1862.

BV# 027-13: *Diary of Noah Collins of Union County N.C. in the War Between the States 1861–1865.*

BV# 028-10: *Reminiscences of the Civil War by Judge Jno W. Stevens: A Soldier in Hood's Texas Brigade*, Army of Northern Virginia.

BV# 029-07: Letters of Isaac Newton Cooper.

BV# 031-06: Rockbridge Artillery Letters of Joseph Shaner.

BV# 031-07: Letters of A.S. Dandridge, Rockbridge Artillery.

BV# 080-02: Letters of John McDonald, 13th Mississippi.

BV# 083-12: Letters from King David Richards, Company A, 57th Va. Infy.

BV# 104-07: W. Johnson J. Webb Co. I, 51st Ga. Vols. Courtesy of Carlisle Barracks—Lewis Leigh Collection.

BV# 125-06: *The Civil War Diary of James J. Kirkpatrick*, 16th Mississippi Infantry, CSA.

BV# 128-12: Letters from James T. McElvaney. Co. F, 35th GA.

BV# 162-04–162-05: *Incidents in the life of a Private Soldier in the War Waged by the United States against the Confederate States 1861–1865*. Robert Wallace Shand, Co. C., 2nd SCV (South Carolina Library).

BV# 206-09: *Sketches of Army Life, Interesting Incidents of the Civil War Related by "X Con. Fed." A Member of Third S.C. Regiment.*

BV# 236-13: *History of Edgefield County, From the Earliest Settlements to 1897.* John A. Chapman. Newberry, SC: Elbert H. Aull, 1897.

BV# 242-03: *Letters of Samuel C. Clyde*, 2nd S.C. Inf. (Terry Burnett Collection).

BV# 289-25: Lieutenant Thomas M. Hightower (Co. D 21st Ga. Vols) Letters. Drawer 40, Box 50 (microfilm), Ga. Archives.

WEBSITES

Civil War Preservation Trust. www.cwpt.org.

Fredericksburg/Spotsylvania Military Parks. www.nps.gov/frsp.

HistoryPoint Fredericksburg/Spotsylvania. www.historypoint.org.

Spotsylvania County Tourism Bureau. www.spotsylvania.va.us/departments/tourism.

The Valley of the Shadow Project. valley.vcdh.virginia.edu.

Virginia Military Institute Archives. www.vmi.edu/archives.

ABOUT THE AUTHOR

Author at Lee's headquarters camp reenactment in Harrisonburg, Virginia. *Courtesy of Thomas Aubrecht.*

Historian Michael Aubrecht has dedicated his studies to the histories of Major League Baseball and the Civil War. From 2000 through 2006, Michael authored over 375 essays on the history of America's national pastime for *Baseball-Almanac*. Today, Michael primarily writes books on the Civil War, as well as historical features for the *Free Lance-Star* newspaper and *Civil War Historian* and *Patriots of the American Revolution* magazines. He also hosts a popular Internet video-show titled *The Naked Historian* and consults on independent documentary films. In the fall of 2009, Michael appeared in and coproduced *The Angel of Marye's Heights* with director and filmmaker Clint Ross. A popular tour guide, lecturer and radio guest, Michael is vice-chairman of the National Civil War Life Foundation and the founder of The Jefferson Project. He works as a technical writer for the U.S. Marshals Service and lives in historic Spotsylvania, Virginia, with his wife Tracy and four children, Dylan, Madison, Kierstyn and Jackson. For more information, or to book Michael for your engagement, please visit his website and blog at www.pinstripepress.net.

ABOUT THE COVER

Letter from Home, Mort Künstler. Limited Edition Print.
Courtesy of Künstler Enterprises Ltd.

"O, if this war was over, you and all the soldiers could come home and stay home in peace." So read a letter from home received by a soldier in Robert E. Lee's army in 1863. It was a typical sentiment expressed in letters sent to soldiers of both the North and the South. Among the hardest burdens borne by troops in this bloodiest of all American wars was the separation from loved ones. Receiving a letter from home was a heart-stirring event for war-weary troops yearning for the simple pleasures of peace. News from the family, bits of gossip, words of encouragement from parents and siblings, endearing sentiments from wives or sweethearts—all provided welcome diversion from dull duties and battlefield dangers. "Mother give me her little sheep, and I will have the wool to make you some stockings," wrote a young son to a soldier father in the Army of Northern Virginia. "Mother says I am a good boy and smart too." Such poignant reminders of home could refresh tender memories in a soldier but could also rekindle the pain of separation. "There ain't a day, no hardly an hour, but what I am thinking of you and the children," a dutiful Johnny Reb replied to the wife he left behind. "I look at your photograph and fear it is the last I shall see of you." For most soldiers, however, the pleasures afforded by mail far outweighed the pain. Letters were read and read again—repeatedly. "Please rite me agin soon," one Southern soldier asked the folks back home, "for I am mity sad and lonesom." In the lull between battles, even amid the ruckus of a bustling nighttime camp, a letter from home was a priceless treasure of hope.

To purchase this print or any other paintings by Mort Künstler, please visit www.mortkunstler.com.

Also by Michael Aubrecht & The History Press:

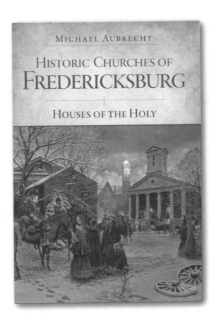

Houses of the Holy recalls stories of rebellion, racism and Reconstruction as experienced by Secessionists, Unionists and the African American population in Fredericksburg's landmark churches during the Civil War and Reconstruction eras. Using a wide variety of materials compiled from the local National Park archives, author Michael Aubrecht presents multiple perspectives from local believers and nonbelievers who witnessed the country's "Great Divide." Learn about the importance of faith in Fredericksburg through the recollections of local clergy such as Reverend Tucker Lacy; excerpts from slave narratives as recorded by Joseph F. Walker; impressions of military commanders such as Robert E. Lee and "Stonewall" Jackson; and stories of the conflict over African American churches.

Visit us at
www.historypress.net